A Book *of* LOVE

By Barbara L. Vanderstel

Copyright © 2012 by Barbara L. Vanderstel

A Book of LOVE
by Barbara L. Vanderstel

Printed in the United States of America

ISBN 9781619967007

All rights reserved solely by the author. The author guarantees all contents are original and do not infringe upon the legal rights of any other person or work. No part of this book may be reproduced in any form without the permission of the author. The views expressed in this book are not necessarily those of the publisher.

Unless otherwise indicated, Bible quotations are taken from the New King James Version, Possibility Thinkers Edition. Copyright © 1984 by Thomas Nelson Publishers.

www.xulonpress.com

Have a great day!
Kennedy

Enjoy reading about Caitlyn

Love
Barb

Barbara L. Vanderstel
Caitlyn's Grandma

With love I dedicate this book to everyone who loves children and gets a kick out of the things they do and say. I want every child to know the Lord and fall in love with Him as I have. To my loving husband Bill of going on 42 years and our 4 children and all the grand-children which we have been blessed with. Prayerfully this will reach the day-care children I have cared for and loved for 22 years and counting. What a blessing children are. This is a book of LOVE. Enjoy.

Thanks Holly

TABLE OF CONTENTS

1. MY STORY 9
2. A SPECIAL CHRISTMAS CONCERT 19
3. THE LUNCH KIT 23
4. MEMORIES OF MY SWEET MOTHER 25
5. THE END OF LONELINESS 50
6. THE BUMPY ROAD 56
7. JUST GRANDPA AND ME 60
8. ON GRANDMA'S DRESSER 66
9. THE GIRL AND THE STOOL 69
10. THE "I KNOW" AGE 71
11. MY PRIVATE DAYCARE 76
12. MOTHER DAUGHTER LOVE 80
13. GRANDPA KEEPS HIS PROMISE 84
14. I'LL RIDE - YOU JUMP 88
15. WE'RE GOING TO THE BEACH 91
16. LEFT OVER PIECES 94
17. MY COUSIN'S HERE 96
18. THE TEA PARTY THAT HAPPENED ANYWAY . 100
19. A YOUNG BOY'S REQUEST 103
20. MY SHANNA 105
21. THE DOORBELL RANG 109
22. THE TALK 111
23. A WHAT? 113
24. MIKAELA 117

25. SUMMER STORM	119
26. TRUST IN HIM	123
27. CARMEN	127
28. BILL'S STORY	129
29. A VISUAL MIRACLE	139
30. RESCUED BY ANGELS	142

1

MY STORY

On a hot summer day in the busiest time for farmers I was born August 27th 1944. Harvesting was on my dad's mind and agenda so after taking mum to the hospital, he returned home to carry on the very important details of getting things ready for combining. Mum's due date was the 17th however I kept her waiting until the 27th. The hospital phoned and talked to dad and because we were on a party-line, he heard congratulations from about six or seven different people. When I was born dad was a little disappointed as he was hoping for a boy. One look at me though and he was fine with the way things turned out. My big sister, Doreen, at home was happy to have a play-mate.

Days went by and as we grew and played together, and entertained our parents. The work never ended on the farm, and a lot of the things that had to be done, had to be done everyday. Some of these things were; hauling water and heating it for dishes, washing floors, bathing, and of course drinking. I was gathering wood and chopping it, bringing up coal from the basement in the famous old coal-pail. These were some of the routine chores. The cattle had to be fed and the cows had to be milked. Hay had to be put down from the loft in the barn. The horses had to be watered and fed.

Farmers would get up about 6:00 A.M. and go to bed around 11:00 after the news. My dad always had toast and marmalade before he went to bed, it was what he did and I would quite often join him when I got bigger.

We grew up very fast and now we have a little sister to love and play with. Her name is Kathleen, however we called her Kathie. Time passed and Doreen, my older sister, should have gone to school however mum and dad kept her back to wait for me.

School was fun, but there was a bully at school who delighted in scaring us. He would throw us into the ditch, throw our homework around the field and run away with our lunch-kit and leave both my sister and I crying with still four miles to walk home. After getting over him we now had to go past a farm house where the turkeys, they were raising, would come out to the road and chase us, with their loud gobble, gobble and gobble.

This was pretty big stuff for two frightened little girls. As we got older I did become the boy dad was wanting. I was outside with him from early morning until he quit working at night except for meals, and of course we didn't miss out on them as everything was homemade. I was doing chores, hauling grain, fixing fences checking cows, keeping my eyes open for new calves born under the trees or in the pasture, or in a slough. Sometimes the new mothers needed help with their calving so I was the watch guard so I could alert dad when there was a problem.

I worked hard, very hard for a young girl but I liked it, I was with my dad. It was a different kind of hard work we had to endure though when my sister and I had to leave home to go to a high school in the City. There was no such thing as a high school where we lived, so we had to leave home at the vulnerable age of 13 and 14, because we didn't have a high school to go to in the country. We had to work for our room and board, so the tuition could be paid.

Emotions ran very high for mum and the two of us. Now there would be no mum or dad to make our decisions, or run to when we needed to talk or get a hug. We were on our own. I remember one time dad set me up to babysit his best friends' children and to my surprise they left coins all over the house. They left quarters or nickels or dimes on the floor on a cupboard, on the bed. It was nuts. I gathered all the money up and put it in a glass in the kitchen cupboard. When they came home they found the money was missing. Instead of asking me where it was or if I touched it, they phoned my dad and accused me of stealing it. I could not believe my ears. That was the farthest thing from my mind. I was simply trying to protect their toddlers from putting it in their mouth and choking. That incident hurt me terribly. Dad and him kept their distance for a long time after that. Dad was hurt too knowing I would never do that and dad's friend was embarrassed.

The first thing we had to do was find a place to live and work. Once again there was a bully in our lives and it was different it was "fear of the unknown." How were we going to live in Saskatoon? We wanted to be on the farm where now there were four siblings Kathie, Gloria, Wilf and Lyell and they were pretty small and we loved them so much. We'd be missing out on watching them grow-up.

As amazing as it may seem, I was walking home from the store. On the walk home, I noticed a mom struggling with her two little girls. Her arms were full of packages and she looked like she needed help, so I ran over to help her out. The little girls were so cute! She thanked me for coming to her rescue and she shared with me that she and the girls were on their own as they just moved from Ontario and her husband was a detail man for prescription drugs. They were living in the basement suite of Gordie Howe's house. I noticed that she was pregnant. I shared my dilemma with her and she took my name and number and assured me that when they got settled in their new home, she was sure that there would be a home for me too. She phoned and before school started up in fall I was now going to move in with them and work for her, before school and after school. Some of my responsibilities were get the girls up in the morning, dress them, feed them breakfast and I'd get ready for school, have breakfast and then away I'd go to school. Right after school I'd walk home quickly and dig right in and do my homework and then do whatever Ann, their mother, needed help with.

My sister stayed with our Auntie Alice. She also had responsibilities, to earn her keep. We had to grow up fast and the only time we got to go back home was Christmas Holidays and a couple of weeks in the summer break. We got to spend time with our mum plus the little ones at home. I used to bring them home books instead of candy. Quite a few hours were spent on mum and dads' bed reading stories and looking at pictures.

Before too long it was Kathie's turn to come into high school in the big scary City. She found the right place very quickly and it worked out very well. Kathie stayed with a family who had three girls, they liked her and she really took to them. It was great to see her so happy and to have her in the same city as we were.

I met a guy when I went to high school who became a friend, then a boyfriend then on April 16th 1966 Keith became my husband. I was 21 turning 22 and we had the most wonderful little boy. Kevin is his name and what a joy was my boy! I brought him everywhere with me. We had moved back to the farm as I wanted to be close to mum and her wisdom. I remember one day, Kevin was already a few months old and I was walking across the yard carrying Kevin.

My dad said, "Barb you are really beautiful."

I smiled at him and said "thanks Dad."

I'll remember those few moments for the rest of my life. Dad wasn't one to hand out compliments. He always seemed to have a hard shell personality. He expected lots from all of us and was quite demanding and lots of times he would hurt us by the things he would say. Even mum was included in this attitude and some of us were always around to cheer her up and let her know how wonderful she was. Mum was born to be happy. She'd have her arms wide open waiting for a chance to give somebody a hug. Mum loved our friends and when she had two of something she'd give one away to someone else. She was the glue in the family. She spent her life trying to please our dad. We kids are what made her smile and sing. She thought her sons were the cat's meow. Mum loved little things, as I do. She would be driving the tractor or the combine and she would imagine she was painting the scenery that she was seeing. She loved to sing and when she was anywhere you could hear her singing. Her dad told her when she sings she was supposed to sing loud so everyone can hear her. We simply loved to hear her sing, she taught us so many songs which I sang to my kids and now they are singing to their kids.

Mum would play the piano. We would sing and dad would play the violin and us kids would dance and dance and goof around as kids do.

Mum loved Kevin. Mum would play with him whenever she could. Their favorite times were when mum would put on her make-up. Kevin would sit on the bed and watch her and when it came time to use the powder puff on her cheeks, he would laugh in fact, he would laugh so hard he would topple over, that wasn't too hard for a little guy 8 or 9 months old. Mum was everything to us.

Keith and I moved into town but still I would phone mum everyday even more than that some days. I had to keep in touch with her, and let her know how fast Kevin was growing up and share just everyday life, good things and not so good with her. Once again our kids do that and how I love it. Mum was getting tired not just tired but bone tired. She was burning the candle at both ends. She got up early, she was out in the field, doing chores, looking after the house, doing her canning and baking and whatever else, it was too much. The joy was fading out of her life and her body. On Aug. 27th for my 25th birthday mum and dad picked me up and we went to a camp-ground for the night and we slept in the back of the truck. Mum had a terrible night's sleep and so did I just listening to her cry out in her sleep. It scared the living daylights right out of me. In the morning she said she had a headache but other than that seemed fine. She was more worried about our marriage and I think that's why they picked me up so we could talk. She was worried about me and I certainly was worried about her. She shared how excited she was that all her girls were expecting babies and oh how she loved babies. Mum died on September the 9th, 1969 less than a month after we were together. She was only 52 years old.

Oh! How could I go on? Mum had all the answers. I would miss her soooooo much. I had a choice either I could give up, or love my husband and little boy and work and cry my way through it.

Somebody at her funeral said we would see our Mum again when we die. I sure didn't understand that however I didn't forget it either. That seemed to be the answer until I looked over at Kevin with his beautiful smile and so much love in his heart for me that I knew I must go on. I was also carrying another little miracle in my womb.

On January 27th I gave birth to a beautiful boy. We gave Kevin a little brother to play with. He was so cute! Little chubby cheeks and since he weighed a few more pounds when he was born he looked like he was already a month old. He was 8 lbs.12 oz. he went through a difficult delivery. The doctor used forceps and a suction cup to bring him into this world. When he arrived he was very jaundiced and although I was able to come out of the hospital in a weeks Timothy had to stay in for another two weeks. He also had to have a blood transfusion so it was a good thing he started out at a healthy weight. Finally we brought him home and what a wonderful little sunshine boy. He would play for hours by himself with a few toys. Mind you when he was a little older he took time taking everything a part to see how it used to work I guess.

Our marriage was in trouble and I left with Kevin and Timothy in June 1970. I took the boys and their clothes and moved out to the farm to be with my dad and my teen-age brothers. I was divorced in October and married in December of 1970. I was trying to fill the void and give our boys a family unit again. Bill adopted the boys and I was happy he loved me and them and wanted to give Kevin and Timothy his last name. Bill knew my boys meant the world to me.

Things happened way too fast and although I was trying to be excited about my new marriage, I was running out of steam, tired all the time. I went to the Doctors and at that time they didn't recognize depression. It was a very long time until I was diagnosed with just that. This lasted way too long and once again I was scared, not for me, but for my family.

In the meantime I got pregnant. In 1972, and we had our wee little precious girl on March 2nd. She was a darling however she had one challenge she was born with one hand. Her right arm stopped growing at the elbow early on in my pregnancy. Her name is Larissa and we walked through many emotions with her, trying and determined to do the best we could for her. I was hurting big time, I felt guilty, although I had no reason to. I simply didn't want to see her hurting. How I love that little miracle girl and she is precious to be sure.

Once again I was really missing Mum. Mum would know what to say to me. The depression worsened and I was doctoring all the time for many months. We moved to Lanigan when Larissa was only 6 months old. Bill was working in the

Potash Mine there. Bill's mother looked after our three children for awhile. I don't know how long, I just know I was too sick to have them with me. I was feeling a little better so back we came to the home base, the farm where I grew up, apparently this is the best thing to do. We were encouraged to bring me back to the farm home. Go back to your roots was the rule of thumb. We lived with dad for awhile then he moved out and sure thing I got pregnant again. Now it's 1976 and we had a little girl on January 19th same day as Bill's Mom's birthday, so everybody was happy. Yvonne is her name and what a blessing she is. She was our baby so we tried to keep her that way for quite awhile however kids grow up. The bigger kids just loved her and of course so did Bill and I.

When Yvonne was three we moved to Killarney, Mb. This is where we live now. I stayed home and looked after Yvonne while Kevin, Timothy and Larissa went to school. I also became an entrepreneur to keep me busy and excited about moving ahead. Bill was a Manager at Co-Op Implements and his job kept him there most of the time. He was drinking and smoking which was not good for the rest of the family. My responsibilities grew in leaps and bounds as I had to be everywhere all the time. Money was short and although I loved Bill I was feeling overwhelmed. The children were missing relatives and friends back home and I had to try to comfort them. I was always there for them, I would listen to their stories from school, I'd read to them, I would hold them, and when I could- I'd buy them something special that they wanted. I wanted to do that. That was as good for me as it was for them. The kids and I were always very close. Kevin was the oldest and was exceptionally good to me and his siblings.

When they all were in school I went to work. I worked at a restaurant, Chicken Delight and I cleaned a dear couples' house. Their names were Nick and Julie Olynyk. I loved them very much. They were my up-line in our Amway business. I worked at a Video Store, plus sold Electrolux Vacuums at one time in my life.

Robin Thomson, a dear friend, who worked with me at Chicken Delight, got married. Not too long after that they were expecting their first baby. When the time came for her to leave their baby boy with someone she panicked. I told her I will quit work and you can bring your baby to me and come and see him whenever you wish. She liked that and the news spread around town and other people asked me if I would look after their children. On and on it went. I became a child-care giver and loved it and they loved me. My kids left to get on with their own lives and I filled up our home with love and laughter, learning and experiencing very good times with other people's children.

I gave my life to the Lord in March of 1996. My life was different from that time on. I knew who was in charge of my life and it wasn't me. I went through some valley days however I had a hope that things would get better. I was also praying for my dad that he would learn to love the Lord and depend on Him when the times got tough. I was very happy when he decided to do just that. He died last year Jan. 25th /09 and now he will be with mum, and with Jesus.

Kids grow up as we all know and most of the families that I looked after, put their last child in school, or some have moved away so I've been very lonely. As of the last school year I have only had one or two children here instead of six or seven some days. I have been praying and asking God to fill my days with something challenging and exciting and guess what? He did. On Jan.10, 2010 a pamphlet came in the mail for my husband and he said it was garbage. I was suppose to throw it away, however it had something to do with children so I looked inside it and got excited. I filled it out wrote a story to get it evaluated and replaced Bill's name with my name. It was mailed and I waited to see what would happen.

Evelyn, from the Children's Institute phones me and says, "Congratulations Barbara."

I said "What for?"

She said "We liked your story "Home Sweet Home" Evelyn said, I would be getting a package in the mail offering enrollment so I could learn to be a children's writer. I would be given a professional author to teach me and guide me through the tough stuff. I was so excited I signed up right there on the phone, while I was talking to Evelyn.

I received a letter from Sheila, my teacher, author, editor and the materials I needed for the course. It looks like we are in for a long wonderful ride. I won't have time to feel sorry for myself. I'll just be learning and moving on with my life. My husband is too busy and too occupied doing his own thing so it's my turn to fly with God's help and Sheila's.

I know this story is long however there is a lot of life to talk about when I am 65 years young. I have been watching over and loving other people's kids for 20 years already. I miss them. We did everything together and children are so much fun. Bill and I have 4 kids and 5 grand-daughters and counting. There will be two marriages soon Yvonne will marry Glenn in September so we'll gain another grand-daughter plus our son Timothy just got engaged and his fiancée Sherri has two kids a boy Gregory and his sister Kara. Happy days are here again.

Thanks Sheila it would be fun to meet you face to face but never the less, I sure do appreciate your help and the time you will give to me in this course through the mail. God Bless you. I have to do the rest of the 1st assignment.

Right now, I am making a roast, potatoes and gravy, carrots and yorks for my husband when he gets home at 6:30. Talk to you soon.

Here comes the biggest fun journey in my life. Praise God!

2

A SPECIAL CHRISTMAS CONCERT

What was a Christmas concert like in the 1950's? It is quite different from the way it is now. There was a one-room schoolhouse with the furnace and the coal and wood room downstairs. Our school was called Olicana and it was nestled in trees in the bald prairie of Cheviot, Saskatchewan. One teacher taught grades 1-8. The high school grades were taught by correspondence.

That is hard to believe isn't it, as now there are so many kids and so many teachers and so many opportunities we didn't have then?

At this time when we planned our Christmas Concert, it was a very big event. All the farm families were involved.

The one teacher, Mrs. Cummins planned the concert and the play. She had two sons of her own. She made sure that every child had a part in the play. She would introduce the children separately and give the audience a "quick peek" of how special he or she was. The props were all made by the dad's in the community and any sewing or frills needed for the concert was the moms' job. The coffee, tea and lunch after the concert were also the family's contribution. Pint size glass bottles of milk were available for the children to drink that night.

Horses and sleighs were one of the means of transportation. There was a barn for the horses to stay warm in while we were in the school.

Families generally had one car. The roads were much to be desired. Snow drifts and snow banks were in the ditches and the roads. A little trail, would lead us home.

There were no rules as far as how many can be in the car at one time. Seat belts and car seats were unheard of. The smallest child in the car would flip over the front seat and plunk themselves on mom's lap in order to keep warm.

We were dressed warm with the one-piece white underwear, with the flap in the back, and the long brown cotton stockings that went over top of the underwear. Our regular clothes were on top of that and then ski-pants and a parka and warm mitts and a hat. We wore over-shoes to keep our feet warm and dry.

The North wind howled and the temperature was around -30 F for weeks at a time. It was so cold the car heater could not keep us warm. The wind-shield was covered in packed-snow and ice. This made it almost impossible to see out. This was a big responsibility for the driver of the car who had their family and probably others in the car.

When the weather was really bad the transportation of choice would be a horse and cutter. This is way we would come home. A little stove was on the floor of the cutter where the kids would each try to get their cold hands over it, to warm up. A fight was on then. Oh yes! Kids we did have our disagreements too just like you.

Before we even got in the car to go to the concert, the furnace in the basement had to be stoked with big chunks of wood and a good measure of coal so we wouldn't come back to a frozen home.

When was the last time you guys came home to a cold house? Probably that has never happened to you, which is a good thing.

The excitement of participating in the concert put the jitters in some of our stomachs.

The teacher made sure we knew our lines and when to say them, however it was still a real responsibility to do things right and to thrill our parents and our teacher.

The tree was all decorated by the children of all ages ahead of time. Balls and shapes and mementos of all kinds were proudly displayed on the tree. Brightly colored lights with a beautiful big star at the top of the tree put on the finishing touch. Presents for every child were around the base of the tree. The excitement was building.

"God Save the King" and "Oh Canada" were sung before the concert started and a short prayer was said.

Every child in the skit held a decorated letter and they would say their line or lines pertaining to the Christmas story. Other children would participate by saying a poem or singing a Christmas song. Sometimes the smallest children would do a special dance while the teacher played the piano for them.

        C is for the Christ child born upon this day
        H is for herald angels in the night
        R means our Redeemer
        I means Israel
        S is for the star that shone so bright
        T is for three wise men. They who travelled far
        M is for the manger where He lay
        A is for all He stands for
        S means shepherds came

And that's why there's a Christmas Day!

This is the play they performed on that cold blustery night.

H0! HO! HO! Santa Claus would come running in after the concert was over. The excitement and screaming was loud and real. Every child including the siblings in every family would get a stocking with a Christmas orange, some nuts and some candy and maybe a little toy. Every school age child would get a special gift. A pen and pencil set or a doll or a truck or something that fit their personality just right. It was wonderful.

After the concert we would sit around and visit and laugh and encourage one another. The snack which the mothers' brought was always tasty. Egg salad, or roast beef sandwiches were appreciated by all, short and tall. Homemade Christmas cake or carrot muffins or chocolate squares were some of the yummy deserts we enjoyed.

Little babies and small children were fast asleep in the back corner of the room. The desks had been all pushed together to make a strong foundation for the little ones. As the parents came in they would stretch their coats and scarves on the desks. The little children had a safe and a cozy place to sleep wrapped in their blankets sleeping on other people's coats, while the concert was on.

The mom's and dad's were free to watch and enjoy their older children.

Around 10:30 p.m. we would say our goodbyes and our parents would gather up the sleeping children and the rest of us would go home feeling tired but happy. The way you feel after participating in your own special Christmas Concert.

That's quite a difference, right? However all Christmas Concerts are special. You are special too no matter how or where you participate. It is so important to the out-come of the concert. Enjoy! Merry Christmas to everybody out there. Remember the true meaning of Christmas and share it with others.

3

THE LUNCH KIT

On a hot summer day in August 1952 in the little town of Cheviot, Saskatchewan while sitting on the porch steps of our home I watched nature in its finest form. Birds were flying in amongst the poplar trees, chickens were clucking as they pecked the ground for food; a barn swallow was swooping down at our grey fluffy farm cat in the machine shed. I looked up and a white vapor trail was stretched across the blue sky. I was almost lost in the beauty of things happening around me when I remembered I was suppose to be in the kitchen helping Mom put together a lunch for dad who was in the field

The smell of the freshly cut brown bread made my mouth water. Mom had sliced the bread for sandwiches and had already brought out the sliced cold roast beef... I covered the slices of bread on the one side with the meat and put some hot mustard on the other side. I closed up the sandwiches. Mom handed me a piece of wax paper to wrap up the sandwiches. What else would dad want to eat? I got some squares of rice crispy treat. This felt sticky to the touch but tasted oh so sweet. I ran downstairs to get a rosy red apple from the box of apples and charged up the stairs to put it in his lunch kit. Two big crunchy ginger snap cookies that smelled like cinnamon and other spices were included... We got out the silver thermos and filled it with ice cold lemonade, a little on the sour side. Mom made some banana muffins this morning. I put in one of those... Before closing the lunch kit I wrote dad a note saying "I love you daddy. Mom picked up the lunch kit and walked with me out on the step. The screen door slammed behind us.

Mom reached for me and gave me a hug. She buried her face in my light brown hair and then turned me around so she could look into my innocent blue eyes.

She whispered, "You'll do just great and your daddy will be so glad to see you."

Mom smelled like a mixture of flowers and baby powder. Mum was my safety net, the love I always needed, and a good listener. I took the lunch kit and headed on down the hill. My eyes were quickly riveted on some sparkly rough stones. I set the lunch kit down and decided to take a closer look at these new found treasures. I could hear the ducks on the slough beside the road.

The white shorts I'm wearing with all the pockets came in handy as I could gather lots of stones and the pink tank top was a good idea for a hot sunny day. Down the road I walked right through the tree belt. I turned to my left and could see the combine in the field. The sea of golden grain felt cold on my legs as I made my way to dad on the combine.

What a feeling it so worth it. I got to my dad myself.

4

MEMORIES OF MY SWEET MOTHER

*Y*vonne, our youngest daughter, my husband calls her the "kid." mentioned to me on the phone the other day how much she likes the stories I've been writing in the Children's Writing Course however, she said to me.

"Mum why don't you write a story about your mother, our grandma?"

I didn't really give her an answer as I wondered how much I could remember. I love her dearly and she was the glue that held our family together. She was the soft place to fall. She had such a listening ear.

We started a new Bible study lesson on Sunday mornings at 9:00. It's being taught at the New Life Assembly Church in Killarney, MB.

Jim and Colleen are the teachers and I've known and loved them for many years. They love the Lord. They are teaching 4 keys to "Hearing God's Voice." by Mark and Patti Virkler.

It's great I'm realizing I've been hearing from God for a long time since I gave my life to the Lord in March 1996 and got baptized in the Killarney, lake in July 29th, 1996. Oh I'm waiting for that day when He says Barbara.

Last night at 3:00 in the morning I was awoke with a

picture of my Mum smiling at me. She seemed so close I could almost stroke her hair and I could see her soft brown smiling eyes and a smile that's beyond belief. I tried to reach her to hold her however she just smiled and left. I took that as a loving sign to write a story about her.

Margery Edith Adams (Mum) was born to Harold and Edith Adams. She had a sister Beatrice and George, Allan, John and Harold and Ralph were her brothers. They lived on a farm 1 mile south of where my Dad grew up. When we were living with Dad and Mum at Dad's home place Grandma and Grandpa Adams used to watch for us when we walked home from school. We had a snack with them and they would pray before we ate. Grandpa would take us upstairs and play hymns on the organ as we took turns sitting on his lap.

Some kind of a tiff happened years ago and we were not allowed to go there.

George Rae Allen (Dad) had three sisters Alice Grace and another sister Lorraine who died at a very young age. I only remember Dad's mother (Elizabeth Allen). Harold Allen (Dad's father) died when Dad was in his twenties. Both mum and Dad's parents came over from England during the war.

Dad and Mum were married in 1941. Together they had 6 children Doreen was the oldest, and she was born in 1943. I (Barbara,) was the second oldest, I was born in 1944. Kathie was born in 1946. In 1950 Gloria, was born. Wilf was born in 1952 and Lyell was born in 1954. Mum and Dad worked very hard together on the farm in Cheviot, Saskatchewan, it later became Clavet. Life changed for the better as the children came along. Good times and not so good times happened while they were raising their family.

The worst thing that could've happened to us as a family was Mum passed away suddenly on September 9th, 1969. Dad and the family and many others missed her so much. We missed her laughter we missed her sharing and caring.

She was one of those people you think they'll never leave because we needed her and loved her so much.

I feel certain now though you will find characteristics of my mother in us, her children.

My Mum was like Doreen, my oldest sister with her strong loving ways, always reaching out and going the extra mile for someone else. Mum used to play the piano and sing to us. Doreen loves to play the piano and she can play anything as she plays by ear. Mum loved the old hymns. Although she never talked about the Lord, I know now she was the Lords' hands and feet.

Mum was like me willing to please, low self esteem, very loving and giving and was very willing to let somebody else take the credit or shine in anyway. She would give to live and live to give. If she had two of one thing she would give the other one away. Mum just loved to surprise people and make them happy. I am the same way.

My Mum was like my younger sister Kathie. She was strong so very strong in so many ways just like Kathie. She kept her pain inside and didn't want anybody to worry about her. Kathie though, grew up to want more and was not satisfied with living a mediocre life. A good decision that was!

My sister Gloria was a relationship builder. Mum, like Gloria had a journal and she'd write down everything that happened through the years. She'd remember birthdays as she had earlier written everything down in her little book. Something small but meaningful was what she did and it was delivered or brought to them on time. She loved to bake, as all of us girls did then and do now. We were taught when we were very young to cook and clean and bake and look after our siblings and other little ones. I was the best at that as I had the patience the other girls didn't have. She, like Gloria would buy little things ahead of times so she could give that special person the right card or shower gift or wedding gift or even a baby gift. Both of them are amazing at that.

Wilf, my young brother was so much like her as he was happy for no reason. You could hear her laughing or singing all over the house, when we were younger. Mum loved to hug and snuggle so does Willie. He found the tickle side of life just as Mum did.

Lyell was wonderful but he was very strong willed. He was her baby and she adored him. She figured her little boys were the cats meow.

They were hoping for boys, so they could take over the farm however they were blessed with four girls first. It was a big celebration when Mum gave birth to Wilf and then to Lyell. She loved her kids. We were her world.

Mum and Dad worked very hard. As soon as we could walk talk and run we had chores to do. Probably not quite that young, however we went with them everywhere out in the field, in the truck, on the tractor, on the combine or even out to the barn we were with them and we learned by watching what they did.

Mum and Dad had to plant big gardens as our family increased.

There were always lots of things to do on the farm. One day we were working up some land in order to put in another garden and we ran into some roots of some kinds of plants or trees. She almost ripped her hands apart trying to get rid of those roots so we could plant a new garden of potatoes.

We had a huge garden in fact we had three of them. Gardens need planting and weeding. What a job that was. Sometimes the weeds would get ahead of us. When we would pull them it would take quite a chunk out of the ground. This would give the appearance of us doing a lot when we pulled a few. It was generally very hot. Even when us kids gave up and went in Mum would stay out and do everything she could to get a jump on the weeds before it rained again. The gardens were well looked after and so in the fall we would have quite a harvest.

Hauling vegetables in those five gallon pails was heavy. Emptying them and then going down the hill to get some more kept us busy all day. Cucumbers would almost be coming out of our ears. Mum made lots of pickles and relishes. Pumpkins were hiding under the green leaves hoping they wouldn't get noticed. We would get excited about her pumpkin pies with real whipping cream. This was one thing we took for granted.

We kids would so enjoy sitting on the front step with pails and pails of peas ready to shell or buckets and boxes of corn to get ready to can for the winter months. She would make beet pickles and sometimes bread and butter pickles. Canned peas and beans tasted good, but fresh ones tasted even better. We never froze vegetables in those days. The garden took a lot of time however with us kids to help her it would be a lot of fun. I can still hear her tell us.

"Put some peas in the bowls girls; don't eat all of them right now we need them for the winter."

Mum and Dad would go into town, Saskatoon that is, and they would bring home crates of fruit for eating and canning and making jams and jellies. Scalding the jars over the spout of the boiling kettle water was part of the canning process. Doreen got to help Mum with this as she was the oldest. One of our many jobs was to carry and place jars and jars of vegetables and fruit on the shelves in the basement. The basement was kind of a cold scary place. None of us really liked going down there.

Potatoes had to be dug and put in gunny sacks to be put down in the basement. Carrots had to be placed under sand in the big wooden box crate so they wouldn't spoil. We could eat them all winter that way. Mum generally helped Dad butcher a cow for meat for the winter. We butchered chickens for eating too.

I remember one day I sat on the milk stool and I was ready to milk the cow when all of a sudden a cat climbed to close. The cow swished her tail let out a kick to knock the cat off his haunches and I went flying milk pail and all. It was a very interesting time and didn't really convince me to go milking the cow.

All summer you could find mum on the tractor or hauling grain to the elevator or unloading the truck. She never stopped. Many times she would take one or two kids with her and we'd get to see the elevator and the grain coming out of the shoot in the truck and go down into the hole where they stored the grain. She would go to bed exhausted and get up smiling. She knew how much her kids loved her and she loved her kids. She loved Dad very much however she couldn't understand his crankiness sometimes. She was always trying to please him.

Mum would get the job of tightening fences or even fixing them when they were down. I dug many post holes with my Mum and my Dad. Doreen and Kathie stayed in and did housework and looked after the little ones. My choice was to be outside with my parents.

Every Saturday we would work hard all day. After enjoying a nice supper we would go upstairs and get dressed in our fancy clothes. Mum would play the piano and Dad would play the violin. Music written on sheet music, not a book, was how Mum played the piano. We would dance on Dad's felt boots and Mum would chuckle watching us.

The big cabinet radio on "Big Red Barn." station was also fun to listen too. Mum and Dad could dance with each other and with us. We did a lot of laughing and goofing around I can tell you. Kathie liked it when we swung her around in circles and then let her go. She was more into that than learning how to dance. Doreen and I wanted to learn how to dance. When it was time to go to bed in the winter months Mum and Dad would play each of us our favorite song and then we would head upstairs to our cold bed-room. Some times we would take the register out and fight quietly as each of us wanted to look through there trying to watch Mum and Dad play. It wouldn't be long before you'd hear one or the other saying

"Girls get to bed now we've already let you stay up too long."

Mum would whip up things so quick. We watched her as she put ingredients together. She did it so often, she wouldn't measure any thing.

I remember saying to her, "Mum how do you know how much to put in?"

She answered saying this. "When you get bigger and have a family of your own you'll do this too. You see dear, I do it so often that I just put in a pinch of salt or a handful of flour or a cap full of vanilla. I know by heart how much I need. It always turns out delicious. Dad and you kids seem to like it anyway."

You know Mum was right I do the same thing now and I have our granddaughters and the little children from the day-care watching and asking the same question I asked when I was young,

Dad taught me to make home-made brown bread. We needed lots and lots to feed the family for the week. Mum generally made six or eight loaves of brown bread twice a week, sometimes more. It wasn't an easy job to knead it well; other wise there would be lazy backs in it. That meant there would be chunks of dried flour in the bread when it was baked in the oven. Talk about delicious. You could smell the aroma of fresh baked bread all over the house. Dad and I would eat it at night, with marmalade before we went to bed. Mum would make us a cup of hot chocolate to go with it. I really enjoyed that time with Dad.

Does anybody remember the separator with all those discs you had to clean and keep in order? There was always a dispute as to which one wanted to wash the yucky porridge pot or wash the separator with all those discs. It had to be done twice a day as Dad would milk the cows twice a day and the separator was needed to separate the cream from the milk and put downstairs to stay cold.

Another thing we did together was go out in the field and pull out the dead trees from around the sloughs. We would haul them over to the truck. Dad would organize things as they had to be placed in the truck the proper way in order to have a full load. When the truck was full we would take them home and put them in a tepee. Dad got the old circular saw and hooked it on to the tractor to cut up the wood for firewood for the kitchen stove and also for the furnace in the basement. They would haul a couple of loads of coal from Saskatoon. It would last us through the cold winter months.

Mum used to also put hot water in a sealer wrapped in a towel so we could put our feet on it in bed. There were three in the bed so it was quite common for us to fight over each others jar of hot water and proceed in unwrapping the towel that protected us from the boiling water. Mum would come upstairs and do it all over again.

Christmas time was huge at our house. That was the one time when we would all pile into the car and with very little money we would go with our parents to shop for everybody in the family. Kresge's or Woolworth was where we would shop. A lot of thought was put into these gifts as we had to get something nice for everybody. Dad liked a box of mixed nuts from the "nuthouse" so he could generally count on me getting that for him every Christmas. We all tried to get Mum something pretty like perfume or jewellery. It wasn't hard to buy for her as she appreciated anything and everything. The big excitement was picking out a Christmas tree to bring home. Dad would tie it with binder twine in the trunk and it would stick out the back. He had the trunk up, so the car was cold to travel in for those 20 miles. Mum dressed us really warm with our one- piece white underwear, our clothes, ski pants and a parka or a snow suit and warm boots on our feet.

Cozy warm mitts were a must for the cold days.

Often our mitts came from Auntie Alice as she would make sure she knit a lot of pairs before the winter storms hit. The bag full of knitted items was always a thrill for us and I know Mum and Dad appreciated it. Dad could count on some new knit socks to put in his felt boots. Mum looked forward to a few new warm scarves. We would enjoy the mitts and the socks she'd knit for us and a special present for each of us in the bag.

Christmas Eve was always fun. We weren't allowed to wrap our presents for each other until the night before Christmas. The house was a buzz of excitement as we each took turns wrapping our special gifts in Mum and Dad's bedroom. Either Mum or Dad would be on hand to help us cut ribbon or hold the paper together while we wrapped the secret gifts we were giving to each other the next day. We would decorate the tree a week or so ahead of time with special mementos we made at school. Lots of tinsel and bells were put all over the tree and of course a beautifully lit up star on the very top of the tree. The gifts were not placed around the tree until late Christmas Eve.

The giggles and secrets were fun as we anticipated what our sisters or brothers or Mum and Dad would find under the tree in the morning. Mum would have made her Christmas cake months ago and some of the kids didn't like it but I sure did. I thought it was the best thing ever. My Mum would also have baked lots of cookies and we had egg nog for our Christmas supper and of course a big turkey, some stuffing, some mashed potatoes and gravy. She often made carrot salad with raisins in it and two different kinds of vegetables smothered in home-made butter. Fresh buns and bread right out of the oven was something we always looked forward to. We had home-made pickles and relish and canned fruit that we could go take off the shelf in the basement, because of her hard work in the summertime.

Christmas morning started early. We kids would come down and jump on their bed about six o'clock in the morning only to be given a big hug and some kisses and told to grab our stockings and go back to sleep for awhile. Yea right! I don't think so. They wanted to grab a few ZZZZZZZ's or snuggle or something like that. We always looked forward to our stocking as it was packed with a Christmas orange in the toe. All sorts of unshelled nuts were in there and a special toy was packed in there somewhere. I can still see three stockings emptied out on our bed upstairs. We placed them just far enough apart that we would know who each pile belonged to.

Mum would get up while we were upstairs. She would prepare a special breakfast. We always had meals together and Dad always sat at the head of the table. Mum sat right beside him and then the rest of us joined them around the table. We each had a certain spot where we sat for years. When one of us girls sat in the wrong spot they would hear about it from the other girls.

Dad went out to do the milking and the chores. Mum would call us downstairs when dad got in and we would have breakfast together. After breakfast we would sit on the floor around the tree and open up our gifts one at a time. A box of Christmas oranges was a huge treat. Dad only bought one box so we could have maybe two during Christmas day. We made the box last as long as we could.

We took very good care of the wrapping paper; we'd use it again for many years after that. The pretty string and bows were also saved.

After opening our gifts we were to get dressed really warm and go out and play in the snow. There was lots and lots of snow and the weather was cold for months at a time with a good chance of a north wind which made it even colder. When we got older we would take a shovel and clear off the snow on the sloughs and then do some skating. When we got cold we were taught to run around and get warm again. Mum would stay in the house but Dad would come out to the hills with the toboggan or a strong cardboard box and he would push us down the hills. I think he liked to hear us laugh.

We could come in and play with our new toys or maybe play a board game or a card game with the family after we went outside. Our cousins would come later... Quite often Auntie Bea and Uncle Fred would come over and bring our cousins, which was a lot of fun. My favorite cousin was Teddy. We did everything together. After a few hours of enjoying ourselves with the cousins and our aunt and uncle, they would go back home to have their own special Christmas supper and play or enjoy their own Christmas gifts

Mum would be busy getting everything organized for a very special supper where we would all gather around the mahogany oval table in the living-room. Mum would sit at the one end and Dad would sit at the other end and the rest of us would fill in wherever there was room. The baby however would sit in the highchair close to Mum. There was great excitement around the table and Dad always asked us to thank each other for the day and the gifts and each other. I don't ever remember actually saying grace but we sure did say thanks out loud to one another. We would enjoy a wonderful supper and then Dad and the kids would do dishes. It was only fair as Mum made the supper for us. She could enjoy a cup of hot coffee in peace.

All the water that was needed in the house had to be brought up the hill in pails. The drinking water was in a pail in the pantry and we had a nice scoop with a handle, which was called a dipper, so we could fill our cups with ice cold water. Most mornings we would get up and the water pail would have a thin layer of ice on the top. It was always fun to see which one of us would break the ice so the others could have a drink.

We only had a bath once a week as the water had to be hauled in barrels by a stone boat and the tractor. It was then brought in and heated on the stove in a big square tub and the brass boiler. Mum would light up the coal oil stove to warm up the bathroom. Then dad would bath first, then put in some more hot water from the kettle for mum and then we kids would have a bath last. We used to collect snow in the winter time as it was nice and soft for washing our hair. It took a lot of snow though to make any amount of water.

Mum never had an automatic washing machine. She used the wringer washer and that meant she stood there and washed clothes and then she hung the clothes out on the clothes line to dry. When she brought the frozen clothes in they would stand up by themselves. She would hang the little things on a clothes horse in the kitchen which was the warmest place so they would dry faster.

We caught rain in a rain barrel as it ran off the roof in the summer time. We also used this rain for washing our hair. We used to dance in the rain outside at the farm. It was so warm and inviting we didn't care if our clothes got all wet.

Mum had many goals and dreams however they weren't to be fulfilled. She would be on the tractor and come home and tell us how she wished she would have had her camera or her scribbler so she could capture the scene or write a story, about a deer and her fawn lying beside its' mother or the way the trees looked or the beautiful color of the swaying golden grain in the field. She would see so many beautiful birds and plants or shrubs that she mentioned would be fun to paint or draw.

Never did Mum get the opportunity to follow her dreams. There was always so much work to do. She would comfort herself by playing the piano and singing and playing and talking with us after supper before bedtime. We could always count on her to help us with our homework or just a nice chat about anything.

A Book of LOVE

Many times they would draw up plans for a new house for her. When the time came for them to do something Dad would always mention how he has to buy a new combine or tractor or cultivator or truck or whatever and her dreams would be smashed for another year.

Dad would always say, "Next year will be better Dear you'll see." She'd get her hopes up again the next year and they would come crashing down again every year as somebody else always needed something. She would always let everybody else go first with their needs. She would wait and wait for her turn.

Dad never allowed her to read or us for that matter. Dad would get cross if he would catch us sitting down for even a few minutes and reading a story. This would be a waste of time as far as he was concerned. We were supposed to read and study in school. That was that. There was work to be done and how dare we waste time reading.

Bill taught me to make myself read. He gave me a book and a cup of tea and told me not to get up until I'd read for 20 minutes or so. I'm forever grateful to Bill for loving me that much. It was something I wanted to do however I was very scared and felt guilty when I did. I learned to enjoy it so much. I would read the monthly business books I got in order to fuel my Amway business and then I started reading positive thinking books and after I became a Christian I read many Christian books, which I'm still reading and enjoying.

Bill said, "Reading was wonderful and I had to learn to enjoy it and not to feel ashamed or embarrassed or guilty because I was reading." Bill loves to read too.

I loved to read to my kids and the day-care children. Everybody needs and loves a good book. I'm just sorry my Mum was scolded for doing so. Sometimes I'd see her when Dad was away, reading a little article out of a magazine.

So Mama I'm experiencing your dreams. I gave

everything to the Lord and He has taken over my life and like it says in Malachi 3:10

> Bring all the tithes into the storehouse, That there may be food in my house, And prove me now in this. Says the LORD of hosts. "If I will not open for you the windows of heaven And pour out for you such blessing That there will not be room enough to receive it."

I am so excited I know that's what is happening to me right now. The LORD JESUS CHRIST is over- taking me with His blessings of every kind. Our Amway business is growing. God's writing my stories for me. The day-care is blossoming and even our marriage is being restored. I know He will give me lots of opportunities to paint with Sharon again. He let me get a hug from my dad in a vision where dad said he was sorry he hurt me in the early years.

I saw mum's smile in a vision. I even made a best friend at the Metamorphosis. Larissa, used to babysit her children years ago. She told me yesterday at the salon that she would hold a book signing for me at her spa when I wrote a book. At the time I figured that would be quite awhile away but now I know it's just around the corner. Get ready Coral.

I have been reading and listening faithfully to the Bible and enjoy a steady intake of biblical teaching from programs such as Believer's Voice of Victory, Creflo Dollar, James Robson and of course my friend Joyce Myers.

I am a partner with all of them and I have been teaching the little children here about Jesus and how much He loves them. They listen to the programs I have on everyday before we start our day. I often hear them shout "Jesus is Lord"

I have been surrounded in prayer sisters and we attend God's Church New Life Assembly in Killarney, MB. We have been thanking Holy Spirit for making a difference in our town and the surrounding districts. Pastor Cal and his wife, Laurie and their boys are amazing. Pastor Cal expects huge changes to take place in Killarney and the surrounding districts. Holy Spirit is doing a great work in me.

Sharon, my dear prayer sister, encouraged me to paint a picture with her. It was called "easy art" and I had a great time. I also liked the idea that after painting for three hours we could take the painted picture home. We have to let it dry for a couple of weeks but it is an original painted by me. I couldn't get my mind around that for awhile. I could do that. Are you serious?

My self esteem started to get better and better. Anybody I told encouraged me and our kids were ecstatic and so encouraging. Our kids are great! I love them to pieces. Our grand-daughters are real blessings too. They really liked Grandma's pictures. Bill too was very encouraging as soon as he realized they weren't paint by number. I did them with God's help following my teacher like the rest of the class was doing. A step in the right direction as far as getting out of my comfort zone and trying something I had no idea I could do.

Years ago when I was starting to go through a depression I taught myself to play the piano to get my mind on something else. Once again God helped me through that challenge. I enjoyed mum playing the piano and I wanted to learn to play. I now play all the hymns, old songs, popular songs and nursery rhymes. I learned to play so I could share with the kids here. They dance and turn around in circles and laugh and fall down.

Playing songs in the early morning before the day-care kids arrive is something I love to do as I don't have all the little fingers on the keys helping me out. I need to learn how to play with some fluff in the songs but with God's help that will come.

When the babysitting came to an almost halt, I prayed for God to give me something to do that I couldn't possibly do without Him. Wouldn't you know it; Bill was reading his mail when he spotted a brochure on how to learn to write children's books. He handed it to me to put in the garbage. Even that was strange he generally puts what he doesn't want in the garbage himself. Why now would he hand me this?

I took it and glanced through it and anything to do with children I'm interested. I read it through and it mentioned I could just answer some of the questions and pretend I was a child answering them. I was to write a short story without being concerned about the punctuation or any thing like that. They wanted to see if I could get the feel and love for little children through my story.

I wrote about growing up on the farm and I called it "Home Sweet Home." I sent it away thinking I wouldn't even hear from anybody concerning it. Two weeks later I got a call from Evelyn at the Institute.

"Congratulations Barbara. We liked your story "Home Sweet Home"

I was flabbergasted. I started to get very excited.

I said to her on the phone, "You like my story?"

She kept talking "Oh yes, about 13 of us here at the Institute read it and they all had good comments about it." We are ready to include you in our family of Children's writers if that is what you want."

I couldn't believe my ears. Somebody else had faith in me and could see what I could not yet see. I signed up and paid for it right on the telephone... I was excited as she told me about all the literature I would be receiving an English text book, a children's story book with author's that started at the West Redding, Connecticut Institute for writing children's stories or books. A binder with all the assignments from 1-10, a research guide and a book" From Inspiration to Publication" She also said I would be assigned to me a teacher author editor by the name of Sheila Foard.

I have enjoyed this course so much and Sheila is so

loving and caring in the way she edits my assignments. I learned so much and gained the confidence I never knew I had inside me. It was hard to imagine that I would somehow or some way write some stories and now there is a good possibility I will write a book.

It is going to be so hard to send in the last assignment and know that the time for us to communicate is coming to an end. What a friend she is. I haven't seen her or spoken to her once. I fax all the assignments to her and she edits them and mails them back to me.

I know Mum wanted to write stories and books also. It was quite common to find a poem she had written in the morning and stuck away in her recipe box. I now have both her recipe boxes. I cook the same meals and desserts she used to. Not only can I spot the odd poem in there I also get to see her writing. She wrote with such clarity and well formed letters. I still feel comforted just going and holding some of those recipe cards with Mums' writing on it.

I recall mom looking out the pantry window saying to dad "Watch out for Barb she is only 6 years-old. Don't let her slip on the grain and slide down through the little trap door and go into the auger."

I was so little the shovel I used was much taller than I was. Mum was terrified that I would go down with the grain and get caught in the auger.

Dad would holler back "Don't worry Barb's fine, she loves working out here with me." That was true I found my dad a very interesting person to hang around with. He'd always have me do something. I remember how he gave me an old tobacco tin of bent nails. He handed me a cute little silver hammer and told me I could bang on those nails and straighten them out. Then I was to throw them back in another old tobacco tin. I loved doing that I felt so big when I was so little.

Mum would gather all the strength she had to let us be.

She knew how young I was and the farming equipment was dangerous to say the least.

She would never complain. She was just cautious and always watching out for us.

The three younger ones were home on the farm Gloria, Wilf and Lyell helping out Mum and Dad.

Doreen age 14, and me, age 13 had to leave and go into the city to attend high school. I just turned 13 as my birthday was august 27th and school started in September. Mum's heart was broken and so was ours. Kathie age 14 followed suit the next year so mums' heart was broken again.

Mum was still curling our hair at night and putting us to sleep with a towel over our heads so our hair would dry before morning. The big rollers wouldn't fall out over night when she did that. Being aware of how sheltered we were at home, we are now forced to go out in the big bad world where there is noise and meanness and responsibilities, like you wouldn't believe, we missed her, oh man, we missed her.

We had to look around or phone around and find a family where we could go and work for our room and board in order to pay the tuition to go to the high school in Saskatoon.

I was walking down Broadway in Saskatoon when I spotted a woman struggling with her girls and her bag of groceries so I rushed over to see how I could help her. We got talking and she shared with me they were finished building a house in town. They had just moved from Windsor, Ontario and for the present time they were staying in the basement suite of Gordie Howe's place. I told her of my dilemma and we decided we'd keep in touch. She was sure I could stay at their home however she would have to talk with her husband. I did go to stay and work for them.

We were only allowed to talk for a half an hour on the phone where I lived per evening and really I wanted to talk to Mum for hours. It was a huge change for all of us.

I remember when they brought us into the City to drop us off at our new home. She would sing this song. "Take good care of yourself you belong to me" She was very sad to leave us and we were certainly sad for her to leave us there. When you think about it we were just nicely into our teens. We were scared of everything. Getting on the bus was frightening. Doreen and I when we got on the bus the first time we never knew when or how to get off. Finally the bus driver said

"Do you girls live anywhere in this city?"

To which we replied, "yes but we don't know where."

It was an awful feeling to feel so lost and alone.

When we got used to living in the city with our new families it wasn't too bad. The families loved us and appreciated us and we fell madly in love with their little children. I used to do a lot of things with the kids including bathing them and reading them stories and playing with them inside and outside. I took them for long walks and answered their questions, the best I knew how, however I was still learning everything myself.

I made lots of meals for the family and was expected to do the vacuuming and the dishes and whatever else the lady of the home asked me to do. I was learning a lot. I had to rush right home after school so I couldn't participate in any sports or school activities. My home work suffered quite a bit.

I couldn't wait for mum to pick us up on the Christmas holidays. Mum and we girls would sing Christmas songs all the way home. We'd be home with mum and dad for a couple of weeks. It gave all of us a break and we would have a chance to play and get to know our baby brothers, Wilf and Lyell and little sister, Gloria. I used to buy tiny books to read to the little ones. We'd lie in mum and dad's bed and read. They loved it. It was better than candy.

We helped mum all we could when we were at home.

The toll of chores and looking after the little ones was

overwhelming for mum plus she was missing her big girls.

When we were still at home I remember mum getting up in the morning then making a rip roaring fire in the coal and wood stove by opening up the draft at the back of the stove, and then making porridge. Sometimes this caused a chimney fire. I can still see wet towels draped all over the stove pipes as she was trying to cool the pipes off so they wouldn't burst and have our home go up in flames.

Dad would miss this most of the time as he was out in the barn with the coal oil lamp, hanging on a nail above him, milking the cows. How things have changed. Now in this day and age there are even milking machines.

When we were going to high school she told us she was pregnant. She had mixed emotions about that however she loved little ones so much. She made a decision to be happy about it.

Mum was 9 months pregnant when she went into labor at one of those meetings they were always going to. They rushed her to the hospital but when she delivered her baby her little baby son was still born. Every one of us now had been so excited waiting for that new arrival. Now he's gone. The crib had to be taken down. The baby clothes had to be given away and she needed time to grieve. There was no time in her busy life to grieve.

Gloria, who was the oldest, on the farm, had to be involved with all this pain and sadness. She was amazing to Mum. She is a blessing that is for sure. The boys were pretty young.

Our parents were always going to meetings and one of the meetings they attended Dad was organizing a high school built in the country so the younger kids Gloria, Wilf and Lyell could stay home and help out on the farm.

Mum was all excited about her rose garden she planted behind the farm house. She wrote away for different varieties, shades and colors and smells of roses and planted them. It was Mum's rose garden. She was refreshed and at peace when she tended it.

Our lives were changing in Saskatoon. Doreen and I got a place to live together. It didn't take long to notice there were boys around. They were easy to talk to and they seemed to enjoy being with us. Doreen graduated and fell in love with Maurice and married him. Doreen and Maurice were the first to get married. I was going with Keith and he asked me to marry him and on April 16th, 1966 we got married. We had a son named Kevin in September. Now I had more news to tell and share with Mum every night. Mum adored him and wanted to know everything that happened during the day. I wouldn't let Kevin out of my sight, I took him everywhere with me.

Kathie graduated and moved out to the Victoria Island after she got married to Doug. They lived there for several years. The have two daughters, Andrea and Michelle. Keith and I went to visit them in their log house.

Gloria and Nelson got married. They had a beautiful wedding. Mum was happy.

In the spring 1969 mum was ecstatic all her four girls were married and pregnant. She went around the country telling her girl friends, she was going to be a Grandma again with four new grand-children. Her neighbors were excited for her. They knew how much this meant to mum. Dad was happy too.

Keith and I weren't getting along very well however I was pregnant with our second baby. I mentioned to mum, when we were working in the field one day, Keith and my marriage was in trouble.

She looked at me and said," you know marriage is for keeps. Try to make your marriage work." She knew Bill and liked him a lot.

I said, "I would try."

Keith and I with Kevin planned to leave for Hudson hope,

B.C. Keith was going to help his brother do some wiring in their house and Kevin was going to be 3 years-old on the 10th of September.

We went out to the farm to say good-bye to mum and dad. Mum taught me to make jellied chicken and beef in jars before we left to go on our trip. We took several jars with us to eat on the way.

We kissed and hugged mum good-bye. She stood on the step holding her little dog Timmy. She was waving to us with a few tears trickling down her cheeks. I was crying when we left. I was going on a holiday with someone who didn't like me very much and I was wishing I could stay home. The only thing that made me happy was I had Kevin and we always had fun together. He was my 'sunshine on a cloudy day.' He was 'my cheer leader' even though he was young. I loved to have him with me and hear everybody rave about how darn cute he was. Kevin was so good and was getting quite excited about his birthday party on the 10th with his uncle and auntie in B.C.

We pulled into the drive way Jerry's place and his wife Ellen was outside waving to me.

She said, "Barb has a telegram."

I said, what's that?"

She said, "Here read it."

I collapsed on her bed crying uncontrollably. The telegram informed me that my mum had died suddenly.

"What! They must have made a mistake." Maybe it was my grandma, her mother. I just left mum holding her puppy standing on the porch step.

She's waving goodbye and saying, "she loves us and we'll see her soon."

"Have a good time you two. Happy Birthday sweetheart, we'll see you in a few days."

She was out in the yard helping dad put up one of those big steel bins. It was hot and she was tired but like the trouper she was she stayed out there helping him. He told her to go in and make some lunch and a cold drink for them. He would be in the kitchen in 10 minutes.

Gloria screamed to Dad, "Mum had fallen in the porch on her way into the house." We found out later she had a blood clot and died. Dad took her to the Hospital. She died the 9th of September 1969. She was only 52 years young. Mum always wanted to die quickly when her time came. It was very hard on us kids and dad and the friends and neighbors however it was Mum's wish.

God does hear what we say. He heard her.

The farmers around our farm tucked in and had a combining bee and got the crop off lickety-split. It was amazing how they came to our aid.

Keith, Kevin and I left Hudson Hope, to go back home to Saskatoon. My tiny little three- year- old couldn't understand how come his always happy mommy was crying all the way home. I held him and he fell asleep in my arms holding my face in his little hands trying to do whatever he could to comfort me.

There was no choice we had to get our lives together for the sake of the little ones we had.

Time goes on Gloria had a boy on the 30th of September. They named him Derek. What a sweet little guy. Now Gloria had someone to keep her mind off things a little. Mum would have been over-joyed. Leigha came later. I had Timothy, a beautiful boy on January 27th 1970. Doreen had another girl, Mauranna in May to go along with her sister Celena. As the years went by they had a girl Danielle and a boy Stephen. Kathie had a girl, Andrea on March 4th, 1970. Michelle was born on March 1st, 1972. Mum is watching over our children from heaven and I just know she's smiling. Mum and Dad would be so proud.

Dad joined mum in heaven on January 25th 2009. They are back together again.

The divorce went through for me and Keith. I married my sweetheart Bill in December 19th.1970.

Bill adopted our boys and now we are a family again. In 1972 I gave birth to a darling little girl Larissa on March 2nd and the last to join our family was Yvonne, another baby girl born on January 19th 1976 much to the thrill of Bill's mom whose birthday was the same day.

Lyell and Marsha got married and have two kids Jeff and Tammy. They are wonderful. The kids stayed with us when Lyell was going through a rough time.

Wilf, married his high school sweetheart, Mary Anne, and they have a daughter Crystal.

Our own family is growing by leaps and bounds and we are truly blessed. Thanks mum and dad. Mum you taught us so much you showed us how to sing through our disappointments and tears and find the good in everything and everybody. You taught us how to stick together and lift one another up.

Thanks Yvonne for your request. My prayer is you kids and the grand-kids will know my mum through this book even though you never met her in person.

God wrote the book by giving me the vision of her smile. Mum has the biggest warmest smile still.

Mum wrote this poem in my autograph book in 1958.

Dear Barbara,

    B e as good as you can my dear
    A nd always do what's right
    R each for better things always
    Build upward to the Light
    A s you travel along life's road
    R ewards will come your way
    A s each good deed and thought you have
        Brings forth a better day.

Love from Mum

5

THE END OF LONELINESS

High school was not my idea of a great time. The difference between country living and city living was overwhelming. My work was cut out for me. In order to attend a high school in Saskatoon I had to work for my room and board. School work plus taking care of somebody else's children, doing housework and other little jobs around their house would keep me on my toes all day. This would be a good lesson in time management. Friday night they decided was my evening to socialize. It was very important that I get home by 11:30.

Being put down by people I loved and cared about gave me a very low self esteem. I figured no one would want to be my friend. I talked myself into the idea that all the other girls were much more attractive than me and also much more intelligent.

Considering my responsibility now with the new family was all I cared about. I worked as hard as I could to impress the parents. They could trust me with their children. They really loved me very quickly and were not shy about expressing their appreciation. This was a big lift to growing up and accepting who I was. I fell madly in love with the children. We had some great times. We also had some not great times as I was in charge when the parents were gone and the children never took to that so well. School was hard and challenging. Everything was new. Hundreds of kids were all over the place moving from one room to the next room when the bell rang. This was unfamiliar to me. The teen agers were not friendly; in fact they were quite snarly. I imagined them talking behind my back. I just wanted to get school over so I could get home to the little children I had grown to love so much.

Although I was enjoying where I lived in the city, I was very lonesome for the routine of the farm upbringing. Missing my family was almost unexplainable so summer holidays became very exciting to me knowing I would spend two months at home with all of them. Days seem to drag when all of a sudden things changed. A boy started to notice me. First he would just smile at me in the hall and I wouldn't even smile back. I was too scared he would talk to me.

He called from across the street.

I never answered. I couldn't imagine a boy wanting to talk to me. I looked around. There was no one in sight. He crossed the street and we walked in silence for awhile.

"Those books look heavy, would you let me carry them for you? He whispered. It appears that we are walking home in the same direction."

I turned my head to look at him as I handed him my books, and yes they were heavy. I said, "My name is Barbara. " I live with a family on McConnell Drive"

"Oh I know where that is. It's just down the street and around the corner from where I live." We have patches of trees behind us however they are starting to fill it in with new houses.

"By the way my name is Bill"

He smiled such a nice smile. I guess he is not that scary after all.

"I don't remember seeing you before, he said. Have you attended this school for long?"

"No, I replied, I used to go to a different school."

We walked along once again without saying a word. Neither one of us knew what to say.

"Here are your books," said Bill. My house is the green one down the street, just over there."

I thanked him not knowing whether we'd ever see each other again except at school.

The days turned into weeks and I'd spot him in the school yard. He seemed to enjoy playing soccer or football or doing track or just anything that kept him playing outside. He fascinated me as he came from nowhere and was so nice and polite and cute. Yes, he was really good looking. I decided I liked him even if he didn't talk to me again. He gave me a boost for my low self esteem, by just wanting to walk with me and talk to me.

One day out of the blue, he ran over to me.

"Do you remember me?"

I said, "Yes I do remember you, Bill."

He went on to say, "I've been thinking about you, Barbara and I wonder if you'd like to go out with me?"

I asked him, "Where was he planning on taking me?"

He mentioned a movie.

"I told Bill I thought it would probably be all right however I would have to get permission from the people I was living with. I also told him I knew that I would have to be home by 11:30. I gave him my phone number and asked him to phone me so that I could give him an answer yes or no."

He agreed and assured me he would phone me. It was Friday so I was pretty sure I would get the O.K. although he would have to meet the people, who were giving me the go ahead. He phoned me and then came over. After meeting my new family, we left to catch the bus to go downtown to take in a movie. This was a little awkward for me. I was excited and scared at the same time. We talked about different things while on the bus. I wanted to know where he grew up. Did he have any sisters or brothers? I was feeling more relaxed the more we talked and shared. He mentioned the movie we would be seeing and asked if I thought it was something I would enjoy watching.

I said, "Sure."

The opportunity to go out with a boy was thrilling to me. He seemed like such a nice guy too.

"Next time you can pick out the movie."

"He did say next time. Didn't he?"

All I heard was next time so that meant he must like me.

We talked all the way as we walked downtown to the movie theatre holding hands.

After the movie we went to a fish and chip place and ordered fish and chips. The fish was wonderful. It was deep fried and oh so big and crunchy with such a golden brown coating. The French fries were piping hot and I had an order of delicious creamy coleslaw in a bowl. He didn't want any coleslaw. He had a Pepsi and I enjoyed a cup of hot chocolate with marshmallows floating on top. This was another first for me as there was no place like that around home and no real reason to go to one in the city as I never had anyone to go with. It was fun. The food was wonderful and the company was even better. The snack was over way too fast and the time was moving right along so we left the restaurant and went to meet the bus that would bring us back to our homes. He walked me to the door.

He smiled and said, "He would see me at school Monday."

How things change. Time was sliding by way too fast. I wanted the days to go slower as I was having a good time learning about, and doing things with somebody I was really starting to like.

Watching movies, going to restaurants, walking in the park, going for ice-cream, talking and visiting with my new found friend was great. He even kissed me once.

Bill would phone me almost once a week and we were allowed to talk for a few minutes. Our most favorite thing to do though was go to the fish and chip place. The time went by all too quickly and it was time for me to get ready to leave for holidays back home. I was experiencing mixed feelings. I did want to see my family and enjoy farm life once more however this boy was becoming someone very special to me. Arrangements were made with mum and dad. I was supposed to grab the bus with my suitcases in tow and meet them at the bus stop downtown. Bill walked with me to the bus stop, carrying some of my things. I thanked him and was boarding the bus when to my surprise he got on the bus with me. We walked to the very back of the bus where we could be alone to talk and express our thoughts and feelings as we knew we wouldn't see one another for two months. Bill began fidgeting with his signet ring and then all at once it was off and in his hand. I couldn't believe it. He reached for my hand and put his big ring on my finger. Of course it fell off or it would have if he didn't catch it.

He looked at me and said "Barbara would you go steady with me and wear my ring around your neck?"

I was floating like the clouds on air do. I was reminded of the song by Elvis Presley. I was so excited and of course I said "yes!"

We both knew the song and started singing. Without knowing all the words we sang.

"Won't you wear my ring around your neck?
"We'll show the world your mine by heck"
"Let them see your love for me
"Let them see by the ring around your neck.
"They say that going steady is not the proper thing
"They say that we're too young to know the meaning of a ring"
"All I know is I love you and I have from the start"
Sooooooooooooooo
Won't you wear my ring around your neck?"

It was so fitting because in a few moments we'd get off

the bus and have to face the challenge of leaving each other all summer. As we got off the bus, a cloud burst and mother nature was feeling the same way we were. I fumbled in my purse and handed him a school picture of me. Now we each had something to hold onto to bring us through the lonesome summer.

We flagged down dad's car. I grabbed Bill's hand and ran over to introduce him to my excited family. In a few minutes I was in the car and Bill was going back to catch the bus to his home. He shared with me that he would be working out of town all summer and we would see each other when school started again. Bill walked away and looked back and our eyes met.

The car drove away and we knew we would be fine, me at the farm doing things I loved and him working making a little money. This was something that was important to him.

This was the end of loneliness and the beginning of happiness and adventure with my newest and dearest friend Bill.

6

THE BUMPY ROAD

On a warm summer day in September in Saskatoon our son Kevin was born. He was the joy of our life. He was 3 years old when my mom, Kevin's grandma passed away. This was a shock to both of us. The next year his Dad and I got a divorce. I was pregnant with a little brother for Kevin. We called him Timothy.

I was in love with a wonderful man named Bill. We got married and Bill adopted my boys. We are now a family again. Two years later we gave the boys a pretty little sister called Larissa. The children loved one another very much. Kevin was the oldest. He could help out with the others and he loved it.

I was going through bouts of depression and was looking for answers from the doctors however in the 70's they didn't know what depression was. We were forced to deal with it on our own. We decided to keep Kevin home from Grade 1 since he could help me around the house with the younger children.

Kevin was very willing to learn to cook and make sandwiches, and do whatever I needed him to help me with. Our oldest son was wonderful at watching over the little ones and getting them dressed or changing diapers. Timothy and Larissa both thought he was fun to play blocks and hot-wheel cars with.

A Book of LOVE

As the days went by, we realized Kevin had to get back to school. We were encouraged to come home and stay at the home place on the farm in Cheviot, Sask. We heard that going back to your roots was a healing thing, and I definitely needed healing.

With love and encouragement from my husband, our relatives and friends I gradually got better and Kevin went back to school.

Living on a farm meant we had lots of work to do. Kevin had to haul water from the well at the bottom of the hill. This was a big and important job as we needed it for almost everything in the house. The animals on the farm needed feeding. Other chores his Dad would ask him to do, Kevin did willingly.

Bill and I were kept very busy doing the necessary inside and outside work. I was very thrilled being a wife and a mother and all that goes with that.

Yvonne came along which gave us a nice family of two boys and now two girls. Kevin loved the idea of us having a new baby sister for him to play with and watch grow up.

Time went by and Bill got the opportunity to apply for another job. He said, "If he gets this job we will move." The managerial position would be in Killarney (a nice little town in Manitoba.) Kevin was now in grade V111 and he was struggling in his school work already, without any other interruptions.

We found out we would be moving and then mixed emotions took over the whole family, Kevin, however was the most up-set. He didn't want to leave his best friend Warren. They had a lot of fun talking and goofing around together. They understood each other. Things were finally coming together for him. Everything now had to change.

We left for Manitoba in the middle of December. What a rude awakening! When we arrived the other kids jumped out of the car and ran towards the house. Kevin stayed behind and took his time to reach the house.

I noticed the snow-covered yard was very big. Big tall old oak trees sparkled and seemed to hug the cold dark empty house, like a glistening ribbon wrapped around a surprise Christmas package.

Bill unlocked the door and we piled in, anxious to see what it looked like inside. The kitchen was big with a double stainless-steel sink and there was cold and hot running water. The living-room had wide window sills where bright beautiful plants could be enjoyed. The bedrooms and bathroom were upstairs, much like the old farm house.

The school was a few blocks away for the three older kids. Kevin tried, however I could see he wasn't adjusting very well. He missed his friends and especially Warren and I had no way of comforting him. In Kevin's desperate attempt to make friends quickly, he became involved with the wrong crowd. Kevin's attitude changed, he was angry and unhappy.

One day a car-load of noisy, boisterous, rude teen-agers pulled up in front of the house and motioned to Kevin to get into the old car. Kevin looked scared and I was terrified. My heart broke as I watched Kevin get into the car. The tires screeched as the car fish-tailed its way down the street. Kevin was leaning out the open-window looking back at me crying. With tears streaming down my cheeks, I cried out to the Lord.

"Please Father protect our son, help him to make Godly choices."

The other children tried to comfort me. We walked into the living-room and I put a Bible story about The Prodigal son in the VCR to take our mind off things that were happening around us.

Above the noise I thought I heard the phone ringing. I didn't feel like answering it. I didn't want to talk to anybody. A nudging came so I figured maybe I should answer the phone. I answered against my better judgments.

"Hello, Kevin is that you?" I could hear someone crying.

"Mom, they don't know where I am, they want me to try drugs and I don't want to. I snuck out and ran next door to call you."

"Mom, don't worry I didn't do anything."

"Would you watch for me? Mom I'm walking home."

It was true. God does answer prayers. He certainly answered this one for me. Kevin was on his way home.

I put the phone down and ran to the front door to wait for our own prodigal son to come home.

The time seemed to drag as I watched every silhouette walk down our street. After a short time I glanced up and there he was. Our blond-haired blue-eyed boy was standing in front of me on the front steps.

Through muffled sobs, coming from both of us, Kevin apologized to me and said"I realize I've got it pretty good here at home; I'm going to be more careful. Hanging around with the right crowd from now on is something I will do."

The other kids and I threw our arms around him and welcomed him back home.

He noticed the movie was on. He reached for Yvonne, his youngest sister and put her on his lap. The other siblings crowded around him and still kept their eye on the movie.

I went into the kitchen to make us a nice snack. We were all together again and their Dad would be home soon. Once again it really was "HOME SWEET HOME."

7

JUST GRANDPA AND ME

*M*om's driving me out to the farm to stay with grandpa for a few hours. Mom and Grandma are going back into town to spend some special time together. Mom assures me I will have a great time with Grandpa. While driving into the yard I notice Grandma is ready to go. I get out and Grandma gets in after we share some hugs and kisses. We will be back at 4:00. Grandma wants to make a nice supper for Grandpa and her and I want to make a special supper for you and your Dad. You can help me later if you wish.

I stood there looking and feeling sad and lost while watching the car drive away with the precious people in my life. Now I am here with Grandpa all by myself. How is this going to be any fun? All Grandpa does is work, work, work. He won't have any time to play ball with me.

I look over and there is Grandpa standing on the front step.

I holler, "Grandpa are you going to play ball with me now?"

"No!"

"Why not Grandpa?"

"Well young man, work comes before play?"

Oh no, what's going to happen? Am I going to have any fun here?

"Can I help you Grandpa?" says an unsettled young man.

A Book of LOVE

Grandpa walks over to me, ruffles my hair and says, "I would not have it any other way. We have lots of chores to do."

"What does that mean? Chores means the cows need feeding, hay needs to be put down from the hay loft, and the eggs need to be gathered from the hen house. He went on. Water for drinking has to be brought up from the well. Even the fence beside the barn needs to be fixed. That will get us started right son?"

"I guess so," Grandpa.

"Jeff let's make play out of work. Work can be fun."

Grandpa walks towards the barn. I have to run to catch up. As we get closer to the barn, he points to the big tree.

"Would you like to climb that tree? That's the tree your Mom climbed when she was your age."

I nodded my head however he could see I was nervous about going up so high in that tree. Grandpa picks me up and carries me to the tree. He points to some strong branches and tells me to hang on to them and just keep going up. He speaks a little louder as he's making me feel better as I struggle to go higher up the tree.

"Wow! Look at you! What can you see from up there?"

"I can see the cows in the fence, the cars going that way on the faraway road. I can see your green tractor on the other side of the trees and I can see your bald head Grandpa."

"Oh never mind that, says Grandpa. You better come down now we have lots to do."

"Grandpa, I'm scared"

"You are fine. Just go slow and make sure you put your feet on a sturdy branch as you come back down. I'll catch you as you jump from the lowest branch."

I carefully make my way down the tall tree and then fly into Grandpa's strong arms.

That was so fun. He hands me a small silver colored hammer and we walk over to the fence by the barn. Grandpa

has a big hammer with a brown handle .He hits some nail and I watch as they disappear into the fence post.
"O.K. let's go." Calls Grandpa
We walk towards the barn and Grandpa puts his foot on the creaky brown ladder that goes upstairs to the top of the barn where the hay is.
.I call out to Grandpa. "I don't know how to get up on your broken ladder."
Grandpa reaches down and grabs my little hand in his big strong hand and pulls me up on the step of the ladder. We reach the top.
He says. "Follow me."
He opens the door and to my surprise we are in a very smelly place where the chickens are making a terrible noise.
Grandpa says, "It means they are happy to see us."
Grandpa picks me up. He reaches into the nest where a hen is and brings out some eggs When we get our chores done I will use some of these eggs and make us a nice scrambled egg lunch.
"I don't eat these kinds of eggs Grandpa. Mom buys them from the store."
Grandpa explains to me farmers raise chickens and then the hens lay eggs and the farmers gather them and clean them up and then the farmers sell them to the store.
We leave the hen-house and he shows me a big fluffy mother cat. She is feeding her kittens.
"Can I hold Grandpa?"
"No," says Grandpa, they are too small, they do not even have their eyes open yet" You can stroke the mama cat though."
"Come on, We still have work to do."
"What are we going to do now Grandpa?"
"I will throw some fresh hay down this trap door and you can either go down on the ladder or you can jump down on the hay."

"I want to jump on the hay. The hay smells nice and tickles my back as it crawls up under my red shirt."

I notice the cows in front of me and pick up an arm load of hay and put it in front of them where it looks like they eat.

"Good for you, now reach down in the barrel and fill up that old basin with chop and put it on top of the hay in the feeding trough."

The cows really liked that. Grandpa was right. Work really can be play. This is fun.

"Jeff you run over to the house and get the water pails from the pantry." Please Jeff

"Do I have to take off my shoes Grandpa?"

"No, not this time. Grandma will understand. Grandpa went on, "Meet me at the top of the hill. I'm going up to gather some more eggs so we can bring them to the house when we go.

"Hi Grandpa, here are the pails. You sure are strong. These are heavy I dragged them on the ground."

"I know I was watching you. Why don't you take the little pail of eggs and I'll take the water pails and we'll go down to the pump house at the bottom of the hill and get some water."

Grandpa started moving the brown handle up and down up and down until water came running out of the rusty pipe and into the pail. On the way up the hill we saw a calf.

"Would you like me to show you how to get on a calf and have a ride?" laughs grandpa.

"Sure Grandpa."

"Would you please show me how to ride a horse first?"

"Maybe next time we could do that." reassures Grandpa

We were walking and talking all the way up the hill to the house.

"Now jump up there and wash your hands while I make our lunch. I'll make some scrambled eggs and we'll have some of Grandma's home made brown bread and of course some of her home-made strawberry jam and a nice glass of fresh milk.

You say the prayer Jeff."

"What should I say?"

"Just thank God for whatever you want."

We bowed our heads.

I said "Thank-you God for Jesus and for my Grandpa and for the chickens, and the cows, and the eggs, and for the Mama cat and her six kittens, and for everybody else I love. Amen."

"That was great! Encourages Grandpa, now let's eat."

After our lunch, Grandpa washes my hands in ice cold water with a bar of red life buoy soap. He dries them with a, soft blue fluffy, towel that Grandma has hanging on a rod above the sink.

"Where are you going now Grandpa?"

"I'm going to sit down in this nice big brown wooden chair and have a nap."

Grandpa sat down and held out his arms for me to run into. I heard Grandpa snoring so I snuggled down in his warm arms and fell asleep. Grandpa woke up first then me.

He says, "Where is your ball? Let's go outside and kick it around or play catch."

We were playing ball and laughing when Grandpa grabbed me around the tummy and started swinging me around. After falling down on the grass I lay in his arms. He was showing me all the different shapes and pictures the clouds were making as they were moving across the vibrant blue sky. An airplane was moving fast across the sky.

"Grandpa would I be able to drive one of those airplanes when I get big like you?" inquires Jeff.

"You know Jeff God wants you to talk to Him and share your thoughts and dreams with Him. He loves you so much He will give you the desires of your heart."

"What does that mean Grandpa?"

Jeff that means God cares about you and He has planned a wonderful life for you.

The big German shepherd pet dog was barking. I run to the front of the house and this time Grandpa is slowly walking behind me. Mom and Grandma are home and I'll have to leave my special Grandpa, my fun Grandpa, my smart Grandpa. He sees me trying to be brave and not to cry. Reaching for me, and putting his big hands on my shoulders he draws me close to him. He tilts my head up and looking into my blue eyes he whispers Jeff you are a fine young man and we had a wonderful time together. You are quite the little helper. We will do this again sometime soon.

"Good-bye Grandpa."

"Good-bye Jeff. I love you."

"I love you too Jeff."

This time he couldn't see that my eyes were leaking warm salty tears running down into my mouth.

"Remember we have a date" calls Grandpa.

"I remember." I called back forcing a weak smile on my face.

8

ON GRANDMA'S DRESSER

The door opened a crack and two little faces peeked in the dark room.

"Gramma! Are you awake?"

Two little girls dressed in their fuzzy pajamas entered the dark room. "

"Yes girls Grandma has been waiting for you."

Juliana turned on the light, boy was that bright! Caitlyn and Juliana ran to me, and I pull them under the covers, so we can get our kisses and hugs in before the day starts.

"Oh Grandma, Can we look at your jewellery? After that grandma will you read those little Bible stories to us?"

"Of course you can." says Grandma and yes I will read you the Bible stories from that little case. You go get it O.K. Caitlyn?

"Where is it Grandma?" Yells Caitlyn

"It should be right on that little stand in the music room. That's where it generally is unless you girls have moved it again. You really like those Bible stories don't you?"

This was a routine the girls started when they were old enough to see what was on the dresser, or to listen to stories. Juliana is now five and Caitlyn is a big six years old. They take turns looking at the pretty rings, bracelets and necklaces and then, out of the blue, they run to me to get me to help put on their favorite necklace.

This is a big deal, because I let them wear, whatever they have chosen, all day. The biggest thrill is when I let them wear my rings, now this is a big responsibility for them, because I let them know right from the start, how special these rings are as Grandpa has given them to me through the years and they must be very careful with them. I know at the time it's quite a stretch for me to let them wear them as they are very big on their little fingers.

All of a sudden we hear someone calling from the bedroom next to ours.

"Caitlyn, Juliana, are you letting Grandma sleep?"

The girls took off, like a shot, to where their Mother was calling from. They wanted to let their Mom know that Grandma was certainly awake. The two girls went back to keep trying on my jewelry.

A loud cry of help was heard in the stillness.

"What's the matter Juliana?" Her mother recognized her child's voice.

"Mom! Mom! Mom! Cries Juliana. I lost grandma's ring."

Shock came on all our faces.

I said to Juliana, "It is all right Honey, these kinds of things happen."

There is only one thing to do now and that is pray.

We all got down on our hands and knees and scanned the carpet. We lifted up dirty clothes, looked under furniture, checked inside shoes and looked through all the toys that were nearby. Still there was no sign of a ring.

I said, O.K. Now are you ready to ask the only person who will help us?"

The girls and their mom agreed to ask the Lord where the ring was.

"Don't worry, I comforted, Juliana the best I could.

We sat in a circle the girls their mother and me. "Let's pray together. God will show us where it is."

We looked down and there was the ring it was right beside Juliana's foot. She must have been standing on it as we were looking everywhere.

"Grandma! Grandma! Grandma! It's true, God does answer our prayers."

"He certainly does girls and don't forget that whenever you are in trouble call out to God and He will be here for you."

The girls quietly got up and put all my jewelry back where it was and ran downstairs to play until I made them a special breakfast.

"We love you", said the girls,

"I love you two, sooooooooooooo much" said Grandma.

9

THE GIRL AND THE STOOL

Here she comes carrying the stool. She's found out, there is very little she can't reach when she stands on the stool. I'm washing dishes or cleaning the sink and there she is standing on the stool just waiting for me to invite her to help me.

"What cha doing Barbie?" says Brooklyn I turn around and she's brought the stool to the table where I'm cleaning.

I tell her she can play with the bubbles in the sink for awhile and she is thrilled.

I disappear to go do some dusting in the other room. I look behind me and there she is carrying her friend, the stool.

"Can I help you?" she inquires.

I go to get her a cloth. She happily dusts and watches me to see that I'm going to give her a look of approval. She is really so cute and so willing to do what I do. I leave her dusting thinking I can quickly slip into the kitchen by myself. She notices I'm gone

"Where are you now?" she calls.

"I'm just hooking up the dishwasher" I call back.

"Oh!" she says.

I look around and here she comes struggling to carry the stool. She parks it beside the dishwasher and watches the water pour out of the hose from the dishwasher.

Somebody came to the door. She knows it is Bill, my

husband; we race one another to the door to give him a hug. She laughs. Bill laughs. She follows him into the kitchen, knowing he's home for breakfast. We already had our breakfast. She quickly grabs the stool and places it right beside his chair. That is where she can get up close and personal, something she likes however him not so much. He asks her to get down from the stool. She does what she is told. He picks up the stool and proceeds to put it in the other room. As she runs after the stool he closes the gate behind her. Now with her heart broken she puts the stool beside the gate and watches him from the spaces in the gate.

He glances back to see what she is doing.

She says "Hi Bill."

He smiles at her and his heart is starting to soften. After all she does cut her toast into her eggs the same way he does. His heart warms just watching her watch him from outside the gate standing on the stool. He gets up and opens the gate. She runs to him and gives him a big hug.

"That's better Bill." She giggles.

All too soon he's gone back to work. She watches him leave and waves good-bye. She runs back to me to see what else she can learn from watching.

This day is so wonderful for a questioning two-year old. As a matter of fact everyday here is a great time of loving and learning and growing for all of us. Every two-year old goes through this stage and it is enlightening for all concerned. You can learn a lot from a two-year-old.

10

THE "I KNOW" AGE

Day Care open's at 7:00 A.M... I'm doing the odd things to get ready for the day of little children. Its 7:30 here she comes, kicking off her shoes and running towards me in the kitchen.

"Where's Laddie?" The children love my little brown, beige shiatsu dog. She sees him sitting on the couch, wrapped up in a blanket. She still has her jacket on, however she gives him a big hug, and then runs to her Mother, who is waiting to say good-bye and get her hug.

We stand at the door watching her Mom pull away to go to work. They wave to one another and its clear her Mom so wants to be with her own child, as we have a lot of fun together at this Day-Care.

"I'm hungry, I want some eggs and toast" she yells.

I say "I don't hear any manners".

" Sorry, she says. Please"

"That's better" I tell her.

We fix breakfast together. As she gets the plates and cutlery, I do the cooking. She finishes before I do and off she runs. I call her back, and remind her we haven't found her smile. She quickly opens the drawer and goes to the bottom of the pile to get a washcloth. "Let me help you." I say

She says no "I know, I know, I know."

I help her wash her face and away she runs.

All of a sudden she screams, "Come here, come here,"
"I say how come? "What it is?"
She excitedly explains to me her friend is here.
She can't wait to give him a hug. His dad is trying to get his coat off to hang it up, however the two little people are locked together in a quick embrace. The two of them are off and running chatting away to one another.

"I know, I know, I know" he says as he struggles with the chair to reach the cards on the shelf.

"What are we doing?" I ask.

We're playing snap."

I say" do you know how to play snap?"

He answers, "Yes I do know how to play snap but she won't she's too little. Will you play with me?"

I say, "Sure I will however we have to find something special for your friend to play."

He found her the big Lego blocks and some toy animals and was sure she'd be happy with that.

The big game with the two of us started. He put down a card. I put down a card.

I asked him, "Do those match?"

He said, "No."

I said "Now what do we do?"

He said, "I know, I know, I know"

I said" Fine then let's play."

He threw down six cards to my one. The game was all ready becoming boring to him. I put down a card and waited and waited.

Finally I said to him "Do those match?"

He says, "I know, I know, I know"

I said again. "Do those cards look the same?"

He said," Yes" then he said "I know, I know I know,"

I said quietly to him "What do you say?" He said, in a big loud voice "SNAP."

I said "Wow! Good for you, now you get all my cards."

He jumps up and down excited that so far he is winning, when out of the blue, she grabs the cards and starts mixing them up. Well then I guess our card game is over. On to the next exciting thing, this time it's her turn to decide what we should do.

It didn't take more than a couple of minutes and she was into the book box, however so was he.

"We are going to read her book first I tell them as I just finished playing cards with you."

They both jump up on my lapnnknee, as she calls it, and I give them both snuggles and position them on my knee so they both can see the pictures.

Here we go. He wiggles around, she sits still, he tries to turn the pages and she puts her hand on the pages so he can't turn them. I get to read a few more pages, with difficulty, and they are down and running again.

"I know, I know, I know, he says to her, let's play little Lego."

I reach the little Lego men and give them one each. Now the argument starts.

I tell them, "The Lego is going back in the cupboard because you are not playing nice."

There are a few tears however they know we play nice here and share our toys or they do without."

I leave them alone to figure things out and walk into the kitchen to get lunch ready. Two chairs are quickly pulled up to the counter to help me out.

They say, "I Know, I know, I know, we can help make a pizza, you let us help yesterday."

Children that age have so real sense of time. Everything was done yesterday.

"Of course you can help; you can each have a pizza where you put on the cheese that would help me out a lot." I replied.

The pizza is ready to go into the oven, and I clear the table.

I say to the children, "I know what you two can do.
They say "what?"
I tell them, "You can set the table."

Two sweet little helpers rush to get the plates and the cutlery on the table and I supply the other things we need. Now they're in a hurry to eat. They reason once it's made it's ready to eat. That's not quite the way it works.

We all enjoy the pizza we all made together and now it's time for a nap.

Once again I'll hear "I know, I know, I know" as they try to beat each other up the stairs to get into their beds by themselves. I open the door and they are on the bed jumping and laughing. I whisk one up in my arms and put her into her bed, tuck her in and say a prayer over her. She'll sleep for two hours and wake up refreshed and happy. Now it's his turn, he runs into the other bedroom and as he recites his A, B, C,'s as he continues to jump up and down on this bed. I reach for him and give him a snuggle then gently lie him down for a nice nap in his bed. I pray over him and there is a pretty good chance he will also sleep for a couple hours or more. These are two happy little people that I have the pleasure of taking care of.

Great! Now they are both sleeping so I have time for a cup of tea and a chance to read my book. First though I must clean up the kitchen and fold some laundry. Time flies when you're having fun. I nicely get my work caught up and I hear little feet hitting the floor. She runs into his bedroom to wake him up.

"Get up! Get up! She says, let's go outside."

The two of them come downstairs, sleepy and a little unsure on their feet. I hold them for a few minutes until they wake up completely and then outside we're headed. I offer to help them with their shoes and their coat.

The two of them say," I know, I know, I know" so they do the rest. I get to help them do up their zippers. These children are growing up so fast and since they are not my own, they will be in school all too soon and I will miss them as much as I miss oh so many others that I have been blessed with. Until then though I'm just going to enjoy hearing "I know, I know, I know" because you know they do know a lot of things and they are learning everyday. I'm teaching them and they are teaching me.

All the rest of you little and big children know that I love you very much and I miss your conversations and your smiles and just being with you.

11

MY PRIVATE DAYCARE

I'm going to do a little bragging about my day-care and the wonderful children I have had and still have the privilege of watching over and loving while their parents are away. I've had different ages depending on the families.

I've been caring for other people's children now for over 22 years. It has been wonderful. We have a great time. Everything I do with them, they learn something from it. Manners and respect are at the top of the list and learning to love and trust Jesus

I listen to every child with love so I can give them what they need at the time. Sad or hurt children get cuddled. Discipline happens when they are rude or misbehave. This is a time out on a chair where they are not allowed to play with their toys or talk to their friends. It's time to think about what they have done and to apologize. When they have said they are sorry, it's all forgotten.

When I have babies, the children know their needs get met first. Everybody is on guard. The older children are taught to be kind, and talk softly to the younger ones. Small toys or Lego or anything that might harm, the tiny ones, are kept out of sight and out of their reach.

Two- and three- year-olds are encouraged to learn their numbers. They love to copy at this age and they are quite often running to me or an older child wanting us to draw something for them as they watch intently. We sing little songs and dance to inspire them and make learning fun. Letters are made fun to learn as they copy mine a few times and very soon they spot the letters on a cereal box or even a movie jacket. It takes lots of fun practice for them to actually print their names or copy the letters, for that matter.

This is the mine stage. It's very important to teach them to share their books and toys. This is also a great time to teach them to say please and thank-you. They will ask for the same three stories to be read over and over again. They are learning to bow their heads at the table and say a prayer before they eat. Four- year –olds and sometimes younger are in the "I can do it stage." They are encouraged to try things for themselves. I teach them to ask for help though when they need it. They like to colour and draw at this stage of the game. They are determined to put on their coat and their shoes. Most times they put their shoes on the wrong feet.

Everything is funny to a four-year-old and up to their teens. The innocent laughter is wonderful. We should take lessons from them and continue to laugh all through our life. It is the best medicine for whatever ails you.

Five-and six-year-olds and the younger children want to rhyme words. They love to pull a chair up to the sink and help with dishes, or take dishes out of the dishwasher and put them on the counter. They love to help me cook and bake. They keep telling anybody they see that they are big. They go to school either at nursery school or regular school.

Six and seven-year olds love to go to school. After school they drag out every picture, every book and every note from the teacher that is in their school bag. They want to show me and get my approval and reaction. It is absolutely wonderful how they include me in everything they do.

I make everything from scratch here, just like my Mom did for us. It is more fun and the food is tastier. I let them help me with whatever I make or whatever I'm baking. By making something that is good for them I am teaching them how to cook and how to eat in a healthy way.

Some people think there isn't much difference between boys and girls as far as their behavior and mannerisms go. I'm here to tell you there is a lot of difference.

Boys are wonderful however they are loud, destructive, and even quick to punch someone when they get upset. Reading to a boy is interesting. He is all over the place. He is between your legs, wrapped around your shoulder, leaning on your legs or wherever. He moves around all the time and is very impatient to get to the end of the story.

Boys are absolutely wonderful. We have two sons of our own, Kevin and Timothy and I wouldn't change them for the world.

Girls on the other hand are so precious. They play quieter and love to sit still on your lap as you read to them. They are patient and will listen intently to the whole story. They love to be cuddled and have their feet or back rubbed anytime. They really like playing with hair. I had my hair brushed and played with so many times through the years by the little girls in my day-care. Many times I'd go to the door to meet their mommies and I'd have so many barrettes and clips in my hair the mom's would smile. Girls follow you around and watch everything you are doing so they can copy it. When girls get upset they pour on the tears and run away from the situation. They forgive easy and quickly and come back out to play in a matter of minutes.

There is nothing more special than girls. We have two daughters, Larissa and Yvonne. They are the best and sweetest girls you will ever meet.

I've worked outside of our home doing everything from working at a restaurant to selling Electrolux vacuums to managing a Video store. I must say there just isn't anything out there that can touch the fulfillment of having a private day-care. It works great with my writing course and my

Amway business. It fits right in nicely.

The day-care children love me and I surely love them. The closest I can be now to some of them is to follow them in the year book.

If I could talk to them now I would remind them how much I love them and also how proud we are of what they are doing with their life. I would remind them that God is watching over them and listening to them when they call out to Him. Do whatever pleases the Lord and you will get along just fine in your long life.

Never forget how proud Bill and I are of you and we will never stop believing in you and loving you no matter how tall you get.

Come and see us anytime. You are always welcome in our home.

12

MOTHER DAUGHTER LOVE

"Hurry up" says the mother to her five- year- old daughter.

"Why" says the five- year- old, who was taking her time eating her breakfast.

"Mom's in a hurry, pretty soon the baby will be here and I have to get things done before she gets here. You have to go to pre-school and we can't be late for that."

"I know" her daughter replies as she keeps singing and swinging her legs back and forth under the table.

All of a sudden she stops and she's deep in thought about something. Children day-dream you know and that's a good thing.

"Would you please get a wiggle on it?"

This made her daughter giggle.

"Mom you are funny." She shot back.

"This is no time for fun and games" Mom replied in an almost angry tone.

"All right I'll hurry then" said her baby girl.

The door bell rang. The baby is here! Her mom was excited .The tone in her voice changed.

"Hi sweetie, how are you? Did you have a good sleep?"

Her mother went on. I'm so happy to see you. I'll get some breakfast for you?" Let's sit you here and I'll be right back to feed you."

"Get on with it." Mom said to her daughter.

The five- year- old, with a puzzled look on her face, wondered how Mom can have so many different tones to her voice. Some tones were so soothing and loving, as when she talked to the baby, and others were kind of rushed and angry as when she talked to me.

"I'll feed her, said her eager to help daughter."

"You eat your breakfast and then you can."

Mom couldn't believe her eyes. The breakfast was gone in a flash. The big girl was now feeding the little girl. Everybody seemed relaxed and happy again. The times ticking and it's getting close to when they have to go to pre-school to drop off her five- year- old. It starts again, mom's voice changes. Her actions are rushed and jerky.

Everyone knows children don't like to be rushed; after all they don't live in an adult world. They'll have lots of time for that later.

"Get your shoes on please and do your coat up. We have to go or we'll be late."

Her daughter starts to cry and rebel.

This is not helping an already tense situation. Somehow they get out the door. The 1- year- old is put gently into the stroller and they head off to their destination. Both Mom and her baby girl are almost running down the street while pushing the stroller. The baby in the stroller is having a great time however the five- year- old, not so much. All of a sudden she stops.

Her five- year- old is sitting in the grass refusing to go any further. She's crying, tired and very upset. This is her time to let her mom and the world, for that matter, knows that she is not happy.

"Get up" says her Mom.

"No I'm not going, she hollers. You like Danica more than you like me"

Mom was flabbergasted.

"What are you talking about? That is not true."

The child continues. "You smile at her more than you smile at me, you talk softly to her and you yell at me, you play with her and enjoy being around her and I don't think you want to be around me that much."

As she listens to her broken-hearted daughter spew out these obvious untruths, her heart breaks and nothing, no nothing was going to be more important than what she has to do right now.

"Come here, she said, to her very sad daughter, let Mommy tell you something. You are my miracle girl."

They sit on the grass together, both crying. Mom holds her and explains to her that when she was a very tiny, tiny baby she was very sick and her grandma and grandpa and her uncles and aunts and a lot of other people prayed for her.

Grandma's friend and prayer sister, Sharon, even came into Winnipeg and put healing oil on you and prayed over you. Your aunts and uncles circled around your bassinette and sang songs of love and encouragement to you.

These were songs I used to sing to them when they were little.

Juliana they had you on a big long prayer chain circulating in Killarney and Winnipeg. Juliana Jesus healed you. It was a miracle so we call you our miracle baby."

Let me tell you something, Mommy does get overwhelmed sometimes with everything that goes on in my life; however, it has nothing to do with you. The baby belongs to another mommy & daddy. You and your older sister belong to your daddy and me. We love you very, very much. There is nothing more important to me than your Daddy your sister and you. You are my baby girl."

Her Mother went on to remind her of her love for her.

"You know how much fun we have together. We read stories. I let you play for a long time in the bathtub. We laugh and snuggle lots with your sister. We sing all the songs that my mommy sang to me. I take you shopping, and take you out for lunch. We go to the park as a family and you visit with your friends."

You know how many pictures I take of you two, the reason you are learning how to swim is because I love you so much and want you to learn how to be safe in the water.

"Now I guess we better get up and get you to pre-school or your teacher will be worried about you and you know she loves you too. So many people love you."

They get up and give each other big kisses and hugs in fact lots of kisses, and with a smile on both their faces they walk to the stroller to find the baby fast asleep. On they walk to the pre-school. Mom is realizing that they will be late, quite late, however that will not matter.

First things first. Juliana has to know how much she is loved and how precious she is to her Mommy now and forever.

They walk slowly to the school pushing the stroller together.

The teacher meets them and understands mom's explanation of their tardiness. She gives both of them big hugs and assures them that what happened to- day was the best learning experience ever for Juliana and her mother.

13

GRANDPA KEEPS HIS PROMISE

What did you say Grandpa?
"I said, "One day I will take you fishing."
"Grandpa really?" replied an almost too excited Caitlyn.
"Grandma! Grandma! Grandma," shouts Caitlyn, "Grandpa said he would take us fishing."
"That's great." I said, as I drew her close to me to give her a reassuring hug. When is this happening? Did grandpa say when? Caitlyn did Grandpa say when?"
He said, "tomorrow after work, maybe.
I knew she was too excited to let this pass. I left Bill a note in the morning. Bill was up hours before me, and I had to make sure he knew the date and the time. I want him to realize how extremely excited she is at the thought of possibly going fishing with her Grandpa and riding out there with him in his blue truck. It was fine with Bill. He will take Caitlyn and her sister Juliana right after work before supper. We agreed on this plan and so now we were ready to share the new news with Larissa (their Mom) and her daughters Caitlyn and Juliana.
The day at the day-care was going slow for the girls as they anticipate their time with Grandpa, a rare occurrence.
As I was washing dishes a young girl comes up to me

wraps her arms around my waist and in a quiet little voice said, "Grandma, do you really think grandpa will take us fishing?"

I give her a big hug. "Caitlyn I said, "You know what? This is one thing your Grandpa does is keep his word. When your Grandpa says he will take you fishing you can count on it. He will take you fishing today after he is done work and after the kids here at the day-care have gone home."

"Caitlyn, this is how it is going to be. Around 5:00 your Grandpa will be home and I'll stay here to organize supper and you and your Mom and your younger sister can go fishing in Killarney Lake until 6:30. At this time you will pack up your things and come home for hamburgers which your grandpa will cook on the barbecue.

"Now you go outside and have more fun playing with the kids. They will be going home in a few hours and the time will go a lot faster when you get your mind on other things."

The time moves through the day. Before you know it is 4:45.

Here comes Caitlyn. "What time is it Grandma?"

"Almost time to go, I reply. Get ready to go. Tell your sister to get ready. Don't forget to remind mom to bring her camera. Grandpa is home. I see the blue truck just pulling up."

Caitlyn's is out the door, and climbs into the truck to sit beside Grandpa. Juliana jumps in the car with her Mommy. I watch them leave without me. I am running to the street to see which way they are going. Oh good! They are turning right. I know now where they are heading. I come back to the house to do some organizing and arranging and as I sit enjoying, my freshly made blackberry tea, I jump up. Grabbing my car keys I head off to the Lake where the action is. I can't imagine me missing Caitlyn getting her first fish. I catch myself smiling as I know they will be surprised to see me.

Grandma! Grandma! Grandma! I hear as they recognize the car. My husband gives me a friendly wave. I know now I made the right decision to follow them.

The weather is beautiful. There is a slight breeze. The trees are green and full and you can see the reflection in the calm blue water. God's goodness is all around us.

As I get out of the car Larissa hands me a video camera. She has the camera. We watch as two excited girls are fishing for the first time with their grandpa. I walk closer to them and Caitlyn wants me to take a turn at catching a fish. I throw out the line and reel it back in. No fish.

"Here you go, I say, give it to Juliana or someone else."

Larissa tries. Still there is no fish to be seen. Bill is throwing out the line and the girls take turns reeling it back in. Caitlyn is getting anxious. She wants to pull in a fish.

I am sitting on the flat rock beside the water and video taping the excitement on the dock. Bill, our daughter Larissa and her two daughters are having the best time fishing. All of a sudden we hear.

"Grandpa, says Caitlyn, there is something heavy on my line."

"Maybe you've got your line caught in some reeds, replies a calm Grandpa.

"I don't think so. Says Caitlyn, I think it's a fish."

"Grandpa Grandpa! Grandpa! Look! It is a fish. I caught a fish, my first fish. What kind is it Grandpa?"

"That is a jack fish, or another name for it is northern pike, he answers, however it is too small, we have to throw it back in the lake."

She is doing the happy dance on the dock. Screaming and yelling and laughing. She is so happy that Grandpa is even letting her hold the fish. Mom's busy taking pictures and Juliana, well, this does not impress her at all. She's happy for Caitlyn but that's it.

Grandpa puts the fish back in the water and they are

A Book of LOVE

watching it swim away.

"O.K. it is 6:30 we must go home now. Bill gets in his truck. Larissa and Juliana get in the car and Caitlyn, gets in the car with me. This was the first time she is riding in the car with me. The three vehicles are driving one behind the other. We are now very hungry and in a hurry to be going home and enjoying home-made hamburgers, and the other things I planned earlier for supper.

What a wonderful day, the Lord blessed us with. Caitlyn did get her fish. Now she can phone her Papa, who is at home in Winnipeg working the night shift, and she will share the exciting news with him.

14

I'LL RIDE - YOU JUMP

"Grandpa," said a rather shy little girl.
"Yes Lindsay," said Grandpa
"Caitlyn and Juliana often talk about how much fun they had with you when you took them fishing" replied Lindsay.

"What's the matter," said her Grandpa, do you want me to take you girls fishing too."

"No Grandpa!" said Lindsay.

Ashley chimed in "she wants you to go biking with us."

"I don't see a problem with that, but where are your bikes?"

"Mom and Dad packed them in the camper so we could go biking while we are here visiting with you and Grandma in Killarney." Two excited girls shouted at the same time.

"Where are your Mom and Dad right now?" I asked them.

"They've gone to visit some friends but the camper is open we can get our bikes out Grandpa. You can help us can't you Grandpa?"

"Absolutely." said their surprised Grandpa.

"Let's go get them Grandpa."

"What about Ashley? She's not very old. How old are you Ashley?"

"I'm old Grandpa, I'm three I'll be four in October.

"WOW! That is old isn't it?"

"Lindsay, how old are you?"

"Silly Grandpa, you know I just turned nine."

"Your Grandma takes care of those things, I just enjoy you kids at every age, the same way your Grandma does."

"Here are your bikes. Are you ready to go on a long ride now?"

"Is Grandma coming with us?" asks a concerned Ashley.

"No, your Grandma likes to go on long walks; she doesn't like riding her bike."

I run in and grab the camera. Two excited little girls are experiencing a thrill of their life. They are going on a bike ride with Grandpa.

"Hi Grandma, Look at us! shouts Lindsay, as she encourages her little sister to get on her pink bike and follow them."

They go slow. Ashley is nervous however she tries to keep up with her sister and her Grandpa. She looks back at me and waves. She feels big now. Oh if Mom and Dad could see her now. They would be so surprised.

"Oh dear, Ashley fell. She starts to cry.

"I don't want to go for a long bike ride with them anymore; I want to stay home with you Grandma."

"Oh that's perfect because I need someone to jump with me on the trampoline."

"Can you jump on the trampoline Grandma?"

"You bet your boots I can. Ashley; I jump with the kids from the day-care. We have a great time. I jump and they fall over and laugh and laugh. Do you want Grandma to jump high and watch you fall over" Does that sound like fun Ashley?"

"Lindsay, Grandma and I are going to go jump on the trampoline right there in the front yard."

"Good Ashley you have fun, we'll see you when grandpa and I come back from our bike ride. Bye."

"Bye Grandpa, bye Lindsay."

I make my way onto the trampoline, I don't get in as

fast as Ashley, and however I do get in and begin to jump. Ashley's laughing.

"I didn't know you could jump like that Grandma."

Ashley falls down and rolls around all over the trampoline. I'm getting a little bit tired so I ask her to show me how she can jump.

"Look Grandma, watch me, I can jump really high. Now it's my turn to laugh. I'm having such a great time watching her jump and be part of her young life in such an important way.

"Oh look Ashley here comes your grandpa and Lindsay."

"Ashley! Can Grandma really jump on the trampoline?"

"Yes, Lindsay she can!

"Did you have fun with Grandpa?"

"Yes, but Grandpa tired me out. Can I come on the trampoline with you two?

"Hi Honey, was that fun going for a long bike-ride with your grand-daughter."

"She really does well. I think I tired her out though."

"How about you are you tired?"

"No Barb, not in the least, we came back because I knew she was getting tired and I didn't want to carry her and her bike back home."

"Do you want to jump on the trampoline with us?

"No that's more your department Barb."

"Come on in the house kids and let's have a snack and a cold drink of lemonade to get recharged. We'll come back out later and play some badminton. Would you girls enjoy a game of badminton or would you rather play ball or "mother may I?"

"Yes we would like to play all of those things with you grandma."

"Come on Bill, let's have a snack. I know exactly what we can eat. It will be a real treat for the girls."

15

WE'RE GOING TO THE BEACH

"Who is that mommy?" said a curious little 2 year-old girl called Danica.

I'm talking to grandma, replied her mother.

"Tell grandma we're coming out to Killarney soon. Tell her mommy tell her."

"I can hear you Danica," I said.

"Are you excited to come to Killarney Danica?"

"Yes, I am. Mommy said we are going to pick you up and then we are going to the Lake right grandma?" Where is grandpa is he coming too?"

"No grandpa is working he won't be able to come today. We'll have to have fun without him."

"When are you leaving Yvonne? Is Glenn coming?"

"Oh yes! He can't wait to come out there. He says it is so relaxing and he quite enjoys you pampering him too mum."

"That's fun I don't get to do that very often as you are three hours away and you guys don't come home very often."

"I know I'm sorry mum." replies Yvonne.

The time went by and no Yutuc family in sight. I started to wonder if they were actually coming. Bill phoned from the Legion to see if they got here yet.

I told him, "no not yet."

All of a sudden the phone rings and it's Yvonne. I can hear a lot of commotion in the background so I ask her.

"What's all that noise? It sounds like there are a lot of people around. Danica can't be making all that noise."

"No mum, says Yvonne. We came right to the Lake so we were wondering would you be able to come here with your car."

"Oh sure, no problem how long have you been there?"

I guess we've been here for about an hour. It's wonderful here. Make sure you come soon Danica wants to see you and of course I do too."

I rushed around after hanging up the phone. I was planning a lunch, something that would really bless them. The big square old tattered blanket upstairs would be a good place to sit on the sand as we ate our lunch. I gathered things up and jumped in my little blue Pontiac Vibe and headed to the Lake.

An excited family ran to meet me. I mentioned I made a yummy lunch so of course everybody was interested in what I had in that bag.

Yvonne was ecstatic. She hadn't seen so many people on this beach since she moved away. The water was clear and children and adults alike were running and playing and laughing in the sunshine. People were exchanging hugs and hand shakes. Families were playing volley ball or throwing the ball around having a great time.

Glenn was playing in the water with Danica and Yvonne and they came back to the blanket to have some lunch with me. After a nice snack we walked across the highway to get an ice cream cone and then back to the beach and the inviting cool water. I built sand castles with Danica and we had fun filling her little plastic pail with water and then pouring it in the grooves in the castle. Yvonne played in the water with Glenn.

When it came time to go back to our house Danica was

upset, she did not want to leave the beach. She was having too much fun. We left much to her disappointment.

On the way home we stopped at the store and bought her some little thing and assured her that grandpa would be home and barbeque the hamburgers I had made earlier.

I was right Bill was home and had the barbeque started ready to cook the burgers. We had a lovely supper and then she had her bath and went to bed exhausted however very happy. Depending on the weather she would go back to the beach in the morning with her mom and dad while Bill and I went to Church. Around 3:00p.m or a little later they left for home to Winnipeg and promised they would come back soon to have some more fun.

16

LEFT OVER PIECES

Where are they? Oh there they are. Two little red-haired boys are struggling with the bags as she talks. "The boys have their first hockey lesson today."

"I can come from class and pick them up and get them there on time"

"No problem" I answered back. "

"Thanks!" Stephanie waved from the van as she was in a hurry to get to school to teach her class.

Children were still coming to the day-care and the day went on as usual. Cuddle time, play time, reading time. Before we know it its lunch time. We sit there and bow our heads and ask the Lord's blessing before we dig in, (as the children say). After they eat I find their smile, (another way to say I wash their faces) then they go to the bathroom and get ready for a nice long nap. I pray over them and tuck them in. They will sleep for two hours. I enjoy the quietness.

Soon I hear some voices and I hear their feet hit the floor. They are awake and ready for a great time of play. Before we know it, its 3:30 and I drag the hockey bag into the kitchen and call two little boys.

"Let's get started getting you dressed for mom."

We dump the bag and what a surprise! Little short socks, big long socks, pads of every shape, short pants, long pants, jerseys, and two strange looking things (a mask with holes in

A Book of LOVE

it), helmets, face guards.

I casually ask the boys," Do you know where all of these things go?"

"No," they reply.

I dressed them the best way I knew how and they looked fine. Only when I moved the hockey bag did I discover the articles that were left over. Oh no! Time is running out. I looked up and whispered a prayer.

"Please God send me someone to help who knows what they are doing."

The dog started to bark. That was a quick answer from God, there was one of the Dad's who had come early to pick up his daughter.

I boldly asked him, "Would you help me get two little guys ready for their first hockey lesson? I tried however, I have things left over and their mother is counting on me to have them dressed by 10 to 4:00."

A very willing daddy followed me to the kitchen where the boys were standing. He smiled and said to the boys." Let's try this again."

We stripped them down to their under wear. He dressed the four year old. I dressed the three year old. I was so relieved and thankful that this thoughtful Dad helped me. I appreciate your help Harley.

"You're so welcome Barb." He smiled, as him and his daughter, Makenna, went out the door heading for home.

"There's your mother at the door." I said to Owen and Russell.

She met us and smiled at her boys all dressed ready in their hockey gear for their first lessen.

17

MY COUSIN'S HERE

Caitlyn walked around the house looking for something to do.

"What can I do?" said Caitlyn.

"You have lots to do replied" her Mother.

"No I don't, I don't even have my little sister to play with she's gone to a birthday party."

"I know said her Mom however this is a great chance for you to play all by yourself, with toys you haven't played with for a long time."

"I'm bored" said Caitlyn.

"You're what?" Her Mom ignored that comment as she doesn't like her child talking that way.

"Come on now, you have so much you can do. There are books to read. You can read them silently to yourself or you can read them to me, you have paper to draw on, you have the doll house you can play with. The good thing about being by yourself some days is you don't have to share your toys or your ideas. You can pretend and use your own imagination and nobody will bother you. This can be a great day for you. It's all what you make it."

She was pondering what her mother was saying when all of a sudden the telephone rang.

"Who is it?" she calls.

Mom keeps talking. I hope its Uncle Kevin.

She asks again. "Who is it Mommy?"

She hears her mom say that would be great! Now she's getting her hopes up, what if Lindsay is coming over to play with her. Caitlyn won't leave her Mom alone now she has to know.

"Mom, is that Uncle Kevin?"

She was putting the words together between the lines. She'd run away then run back close to her mom, with little squeals of excitement. As she figured it out. She just knew that was Uncle Kevin.

Mom hung up the phone.

"Yes Caitlyn" she replied, that was Uncle Kevin; Kevin is bringing Lindsay over for a play as he has to do some shopping and run some errands for his family.

He said, "The girls could play for a couple of hours and then he would pick Lindsay up after that."

Two year old Ashley was home with their mom and they were planning on getting in some snuggle time and then a well deserved nap.

The time drags. She wants to see her Lindsay right now. Even the minutes seem long. She runs to the window. She thinks she hears a car, maybe it is them. No, somebody else's car is going down their street.

Her mom tries to get her mind off things.

She calls Caitlyn. "Would you help me fold the laundry?"

Caitlyn anxiously agrees to help however it doesn't stop the questions.

"What time is it now?" she asks her mother

"Relax Caitlyn; they'll get here when they are supposing to."

She hears a car. Like" greased lightening" she's on the couch. Peeking out the window, she sees the familiar car in her drive-way. Off of the couch and over to the door she runs.

The door opens and the two girls start jumping Caitlyn!

Lindsay! Caitlyn! Lindsay!

Kevin gives his sister Larissa and the two girls a hug and takes off downtown to get things done.

Caitlyn reaches for Lindsay's coat. The zipper is stuck. She helps Lindsay shimmy out of her coat. The coat falls to the floor and the girls take off.

"Excuse me, says a familiar voice, this coat does not belong on the floor. Please come back and hang it up."

The girls still holding hands run back to hang up the coat.

"Thanks! Now you can go play.

The books come off the shelves; the clothes are looked at in the drawer as they have not been together for a few weeks and Lindsay has to see what Caitlyn has bought lately.

"Nice!" says Lindsay.

"Look what I'm wearing" says Lindsay.

"OH! I really like that outfit," says Caitlyn.

All of a sudden they throw themselves on the bed and they laugh and laugh. There doesn't have to be a reason for them to laugh. They are laughing because they are happy. They are happy to be together. They get off the bed and turn the music on and start dancing. They play dress-up and laugh and giggle some more.

Larissa, Caitlyn's mom peeks in the room. She sees them talking. She can't make out all that is being said as they have so much to say to each other they interrupt one another and yet still hear what the other is saying. Mum smiles and quietly checks out knowing the girls are just fine.

The time just flies by now. All of a sudden there is a knock on the door and Lindsay's dad is here to pick her up. The girls can't believe the time has gone by so fast when it seemed to drag while they were waiting so long to see one another. Larissa gives them a quick snack before Lindsay and Kevin have to go.

"Hurry honey, he says Lindsay we have quite a drive and we have to get home to mommy and Ashley."

Lindsay gets her coat on and the two girls without saying a word give one another a big hug. You can tell by the looks on their faces that they are sad. Lindsay and her dad turn to go and Caitlyn runs to the window. She has her face so pressed against the window it looks like it has been pasted on. She looks and there is Lindsay hanging out the open window as she waves. See you later; they both say it at the same time. Caitlyn watches as the car drives away.

Caitlyn runs to her mom and gives her a big hug and recalls what her mom said about how she is going to have a fun day. Mom was right as usual.

18

THE TEA PARTY THAT HAPPENED ANYWAY

"*M*om, can the girls come over today and play with me?"

"No honey, they are all at their own home."

"I'm sure it won't be long before they will be over to play with you." You really have a good time with the girls, don't you Leila?"

"It's all right mom," I'll just play with my dolls."

Leila runs to her bedroom and drags out three dolls. She quickly returns to the bedroom and grabs three foam chairs.

"Oh hello," says a creative five-year old."

"I'll take your sweaters and put them on the big bed in mom & dad's room."

"Caitlyn you can sit here."

"Juliana here's a chair for you."

"Danica this is a nice place for you to sit."

Leila"s Mom smiles as she hears her pretty young daughter talking to the dolls. She steps out of the room and quietly closes the door behind her.

"Isn't this nice girls? This tea set came from Mom & Dad at Christmas time last year. This tea set looks like Moms' only mine is tiny."

"Will you have some tea Juliana? It's hot."

"How about you Caitlyn, Will you have some tea or maybe you want some juice?"

"Danica you look so pretty today. Is that new?" I can't remember seeing it when we were going through your closet last week. I really like those overalls and that pink top."

"What would you prefer to drink Danica?" That sounds funny. I've heard mom say that to her friends."

"All right girls, here are some cookies Mom and I made yesterday. They are really cool. We have two bowls of dough. One is white and the other is brown. Mom puts the brown dough on top of the white, and then she puts this brown rolling thing on top and pushes hard. It is neat watching the colors mix a little bit."

"Mom calls these ribbon cookies and hands me the top of the tooth-pick container to cut circle cookies out. She even lets me put them on the cookie sheet for her."

"Oh you are welcome, Caitlyn."

"Sure Danica, go for it I have lots."

"I'll bring you a circle cookie cutter from our home if you would like?"

"Oh thank-you Juliana," Mom just washes the top and then pushes it on the top of the tooth-pick jar."

"Why are you laughing girls? It works for us and that's all that matters. Right?"

"Listen! I think Hasen is awake."

"OH! You know I have a little boy don't you?"

"Come over here and look in the crib. Isn't he the cutest baby boy you'll ever see?" The baby Corina is in the other room with mom and dad.

LEILA! LEILA!

"Sh! Please Timothy she's in the other room playing."

"Come here. Peek in the window over there and just picture how cute this is," says Sherri.

Leila hears her Dad calling. She smells the yummy food coming from the kitchen, where her Mom is making supper.

This is a sure sign Mom will be calling her soon. In fact it was her job to set the table for supper.

She grabs Caitlyn(doll) by the back and Juliana (doll) by the stuffed arm and Danica(doll) by the hair and running into her bedroom, she tosses the dolls on the bed. She struggles to climb up herself. She gets up and quickly puts her dollies under the covers and stretches out her arms around them and whispers to her dollies "I'll be back to sleep with you after I finish my supper and do my bedtime routine."

I'll have my bubble bath, brush my teeth, wash my hair and say my prayers first.

She closes her bedroom door and walks into the dining room.

"Hi honey, where were you all day?" said mom.

"Oh I was just playing with my friends Caitlyn, Juliana and Danica.

"Playing all day with my best friends (Caitlyn, Juliana and Danica) is so much fun."

Mom smiles at her husband and then at Leila and they bow their heads thanking God for all His blessings. They are now enjoying their supper together as a real family.

19

A YOUNG BOY'S REQUEST

Our thanks have been given so now we can eat.
Your Mother has cooked us up a Thanksgiving treat
"Heh! Mom and Dad, I'm big now.
I want to talk to God right now."

"Oh sorry son, that was so unkind
Please tell us son what's on your mind?"
I want to thank God for the red orange and yellow leaves
They tickle and itch when they get in my sleeves.

Thank-you Lord for my Mom and Dad
They are the best any boy has had
Thank-you Dad for the work that you do
Also all the times I can play with you

Thank-you Mom for always being here
You love me so much that is so clear
You make good lunches and give nice kisses
You try very hard to tend to most of my wishes

I have so many special toys
I like to share with my friends both girls and boys
Thank-you for eyes to see and ears to hear and hands to help others

Even though we fight sometimes I still want to thank-you for my sister and brothers

Thank-you for the caterpillar under the rock
And for the fish I caught with grandpa off the dock
The fact that I can stand walk and run
Makes playing soccer, football and hockey so much fun

Thanks for my teacher who is so cool
I really can't wait to get back to school
Her loving smile and tender ways
Makes learning fun for days and days.

Thank you God for the BOOK where it says in John: 3:16
For God so loved the world that He gave.......you know the verse I mean
Thanks for this meal and for making me bold
Now we should eat before it gets cold.
Amen

20

MY SHANNA

Here I am sitting in my cozy chair with my text books all around me. I've been going through past assignments and rereading comments that Sheila has pointed out to me. Bill is at work so I'm by myself with thoughts swirling around in every direction. Which story should I revise for assignment 8?

I know that it is now June 4th, 2011 and that means you are now in your teens. You turned 13 today. Where in the world did the time go?

I think back to when you first came to my day-care, and I remember how tiny you were. Your mom & Dad brought you here when you were 3 months old, just a sweet little bundle with big loving eyes. Oh how I needed you. Your big brothers, Bradie and Dylan were both in school and I missed them something fierce.

I loved you from the get go. I encouraged you in everyway, sang to you, prayed over you, and laughed with you and the other children.

I can't even count all the books I read to you. We snuggled and we played.

You grew and grew and were experiencing something new every day. I watched you roll over, then crawl, then start to walk.

When you learned you could get somewhere fast by

walking, then the fun really began. We, the older children and I, had to watch what you picked up off the carpet, what you could reach in the cupboards, or on top of the cupboards.

You loved videos and I always bought lots of good videos for the day-care. You would try to pick out your favorite by emptying the shelf and then look at me with that little smile as if to say I did it, I really did it.

Yes, Shanna you stole my heart from the get go.

As you got older, I encouraged you to draw pictures and make towers out of blocks. Learning colors was a lot of fun for you. You would bring me "everything under the sun," and question what color is this Barbie?

When you learned to talk the house was a "buzz of excitement."

We had a lot of fun finding letters you were learning on books, videos, cereal boxes. It did not matter. Letters and words are everywhere, so we took advantage of that. What a blessing you are and were.

Do you remember Saturdays when mom worked? That was for sure Barbie and Shanna's day as no-one else was around. We would have a nice breakfast here together and then head downtown to the mall or the bargain shop or the park and I would buy you some little thing that made your heart sing and then we would go for lunch to the Erin Inn or Chicken Delight. Very often you would not eat all of your lunch so then we would get it packed up and bring it home for your snack later.

When you were 4 or 5 you were beating me at "go fish and memory card game. What a lot of fun! I taught you to play scrabble and word games after you could read.

How many books have you read to me? What a good reader you are now with such moving expressions.

Outside fun in the summertime was great. We learned together to play volleyball, badminton, ball, and just run around with the other little and big ones that were with us.

Time flies when you're having fun and boy, were we having fun. In the fall you went to school. I could hardly wait for you to come home so I could feel your arms around me and I could look over what you did at school and hear about your friends and all that went on at school.

After school was snack time and you and your brothers would be anxious to know what special thing I'd made during the day for my day-care kids to enjoy. I remember all of you liked ginger snaps. As I recall even your mother did. Dad's oatmeal cookies were another favorite and so, of course were, chocolate chip cookies and short bread cookies.

Shanna you used to help me make all of these cookies when you were little. When you were very little I would put you in the high chair and you would clean off the cookie dough from the spatula or as you got older clean out the bowl.

As you got older so did your wish to learn more. Mom got you a horse and that was a lot of fun for you. You also got into the band at school and learned to play different instruments. It was thrilling for me though to know as busy as you were you still wanted to come over and spend quality time with me.

I remember a big choice you made when you coming to New Life Assembly with Bill and I. You gave your life to the Lord. That was in 2005. You were still very young however you wanted to do it. I can remember sitting beside you and tears just running down my cheeks because I was so happy.

Shanna I just want to say thanks for all you are and who you have become.

You are very dedicated to do the right thing. You talk and play with everybody no matter how old they are or how young. They love you because you make them feel very loved and important.

I remember how I never had to worry when you were outside with the other children. You would always teach them different games and things. You were and are the happiest sweetest young lady. I am so proud of you.

You have some very special girl friends which were here growing up with you at my day-care. They are a blessing also.

I opened up the Guide the other day and there you were. You and your team mates brought home the bronze medal in Division 2. Congratulations!!

It says in the paper Killarney Raiders 14 and under volleyball team travelled to Saskatoon, (that's our home town) to compete in a three day Canadian Open Volleyball National Tournament and you girls only lost one match out of nine. Way to go girls! Three of those famous girls are from my day-care. "Cool eh Shanna?"

I know this year I won't see you as much as the past summer as you've chosen to get yourself a job. That was a big decision you made but good for you. Just think of all the nice clothes you will be able to buy for school in the fall. It will also help mom and dad out a lot.

So now you're thirteen a teenager, oh my goodness, lots of excitement and new adventures in store for you. Remember I'll always love you and anytime is a great time to come and see us. Even Laddie, my little shitsui dog wants to see you.

God Bless you. Keep learning and growing and spreading sunshine wherever you go.

See you sometime after school. I'll have something yummy for you to share with the rest of my special little and big children. See you soon my Shanna. Happy Birthday.

21

THE DOORBELL RANG

A holiday! It has been years
"There is always something to stop us." She said in tears.
Nothing will get in the way this time
Our mind is made up and everything looks fine.

The suitcases are packed and the favorite toys are out
This way little children in the car won't pout.
The snacks are packed and we're ready to go.
All of a sudden I heard someone say "What about Laddie? Oh! No!"

The excitement on the faces was gone
Our heads went down
As we couldn't believe
What we had done

I gathered the children and said, "We must pray."
The Lord cares about our pet.
He also reminds us not to fret
I know he'll bring someone however who will He get?

How do you know Mom? How do you know?
Can He really hear us? Is He fast?
How long will our prayer last?

Does HE know Mom we have to go?

"Yes son, God can hear and He cares about us."
What else do you have to do to get ready?
Don't make a fuss."
Just do what you have to do. Go slow and steady."

The doorbell rang
The boy said, "Hello Mr.
I know you are going on a trip
I was sent here by my sister

I just wondered sir, "would I be able to take care of your pet?"
Mom says this would be the best job I could get.
Everyday I'll take him for a walk at least once or twice
I'll give him his food and water and I won't get him wet.

God answered our prayers so fast
I'm going upstairs now to share the good news
The children can now quit singing the blues
We'll give God the praise as we've done in the past.

22

THE TALK

I'm going to nursery school today. I'm going to nursery school today. I'm going to nursery school today. His younger brother was listening to the excitement in his voice and since he used to do almost everything his big brother does, he started singing along with his brother.

I'm going to nursery school today. I'm going to nursery school today too.

"No! You are not. I'm four and you are only two."

I'm going to nursery school too," sings his little brother.

Jaden listen to me. "You are going to play with the other kids in the day-care." He went on to say, Jaden can I tell you a secret? I'm really nervous. The kids in my class will be friends I haven't met yet." I know they will be nice but you get to play with all our friends here, and Barbie will take good care of you.

"How long will you be away from me?" says a sad Jaden.

"You know what Jaden I'll only be away for an hour or two and then Mummy will bring me back here to play with you."

"I bet I can color a picture or two and I'll do a great one and bring it home for you"

"Oh wow Kaleb! says Jaden, can you hurry? Now I know that I won't worry."

"I'll watch a Bible story with Brooklyn and Carson and

then Barbie will tuck me in for a sleep." I'll sleep one hour or maybe two and then you'll be back home and I can play with you"

"See you later buddy."

"See you Kaleb. Have a fun day at school. I can't wait to be big like you."

23

A WHAT?

It's a beautiful day in Killarney, MB. The sun is shining and it is warm to the skin. I brought my tea outside so I could sit on the step for awhile and talk to the neighbor lady. I put the two-year -old down for her nap upstairs in the crib. I knew she would sleep for at least two hours.

I could hear the phone ringing so I came in to answer it. It was our daughter. She was all excited about finding the house they were looking for in Winnipeg.

She said, "Hi Mom we found our home. Do you want to see it?"

I said, "I'm a little far away right now what did you have in mind?"

"No Mom silly, you can go on the internet and I'll tell you exactly where to find it so you can look at it and tell me what you think."

"Great! I replied. Just give me a few minutes and you can show me."

I sat down in the blue cozy computer chair so I could be quietly instructed as to where to go on the internet. Larissa would tell me.

All of a sudden there was a SMACK against the wall. I let out a scream.

Larissa's on the other end of the phone.

"What's wrong Mom? What happened? Why are you screaming?"

In my panic mode I shot back to her. A squirrel is in the computer room with me. He is banging against the walls."

"A WHAT did you say?"

"A squirrel, I said. A squirrel is in the computer room and so now I am outside."

"What are you going to do?"

"I am going to phone your Dad."

"I'll let you go then just make sure you phone me back when he gets him out."

"Absolutely, I replied, and that can't be too soon."

I came in the house grabbed the phone and dialed the Legion to talk to Bill and tell him of my dilemma.

Ring, ring, ring "Oh No! Don't tell me he doesn't hear the phone"

"Hello."

"Oh hi Hon"

"Hello, what do you want Barb?"

"Bill a squirrel is in our house would you get somebody to work for you and come home and get it out?"

"A What?"

"Honey please would you listen to me?"

I said, "A squirrel is in our computer room running along the pictures and I want you to come home and get him out."

"Barb I can't do that. You will have to do it."

"Bill it won't take you long please just come home and get him out of our house."

He said, "NO! Just don't take your eyes off him."

Well! That is a fine "how do you do" Just me and the Lord now. I run a day-care not a squirrel –care. At least the baby girl is sleeping for an hour or more... I've got time to think and plan how to get that little nuisance creature out of my house. Just a few minutes ago I was watching him spring from branch to branch and now he sprung his way into my house. This is not good. I am not over-joyed.

I went back outside and let my neighbor lady know that while we were talking a squirrel ran into the house. I guess while the door was open. She laughed and I was stuck with the realization that, if it's to be it's up to me.

Yikes! I didn't know where to start. I looked for him in the room and I could see him under the love seat. He looked as scared as I was. I felt mean as he was so small and innocent. I don't think he knew he took the wrong turn.

I said, "O.K. little fellow it's you and me, and by the way I am winning."

I put the coffee table sideways to bar the door to the kitchen. A goofy idea that was, squirrels run up everything including coffee tables. I wasn't thinking that far ahead. I went into the kitchen and broke up some bread and scattered it all the way to the outside door, which I left open. I know his diet is acorns, fruit, flowers, birds, maple sap and insects however I didn't have any of those things handy to offer him. I was taking a chance that he wouldn't call all his friends in or that he wouldn't charge up the stairs and hide somewhere up there.

I looked around the corner and there he was sitting up so nice and munching on the bread. I could see clearly his big bushy tail which serves as a rudder to help the squirrel steer when it jumps. He uses his tail for a blanket when he sleeps, or when he gets cold in the winter time. His tail also covers him when it rains or when the sun is too hot. To communicate with the other squirrels, he uses his tail.

I reached for my camera. Oh great! The batteries are dead. Nobody is ever going to believe this.

I went back and got some more bread and placed it near the screen door. I waited and watched. He hadn't really caused much damage. He knocked over the picture of my sons and broke the glass but at least he didn't wreck the picture. The glass could be replaced.

I could hear she was awake upstairs so I ran up to get her.

Brooklyn saw the squirrel and hollered "Look a squirrel, right there!"

Oh brother that frightened both of us. We took off into the kitchen and I guess the squirrel, "bless his heart" took off outside to freedom.

Bill came home at 5:00 and walks right into the house and says, "where is it?'

I said, "Where is what? Oh you mean the squirrel. I persuaded it to go outside."

"Are you sure?" Bill wanted to know.

"Oh yea I'm sure. That was fun; however it took most of the afternoon."

He looked at me and shook his head. I guess he figured I wouldn't really get it out by myself. I sure surprised him.

I phoned Larissa back and let her know everything was taken care of.

Larissa laughed, and said, "Mom that would make a good story for you to write."

I said, "I wished the batteries in my camera were charged so that I could've captured that pretty little scene, a squirrel eating chunks of bread in our computer room, looking like this was his home."

24

MIKAELA

Just look at that child
She's only a one- year- old
Her blue eyes sparkle
The long blond hair is wild

Mikaela is on the run
She sees older children
Now this sure is fun
What can I do?

She notices kids building castles
Or playing with Lego
She gets up on a chair
And in so doing she shakes the table

The castle comes down and the sound
Of blocks falling everywhere
Makes her not so popular with the kids around
She giggles and gets down from the chair.

She looks across the room
A little boy is building a puzzle
Mikaela hurries over to push it off onto the floor
Then runs into the kitchen to get the broom

She spots her little brother with his bottle
And makes it her job to take it away
She doesn't understand why he is crying
She sits down beside him and wants him to play

Jumping up from a sitting position
She runs into the kitchen and tries to reach her cup
She gets a cold bath
She didn't realize the cup was filled up.

This sweet little person has so much love
She runs and dances and sings in her own little ways
A beautiful little girl growing up so fast
I'm remembering how tiny and helpless she was in the past

There she goes she's playing with my shoes
Slipping her tiny feet in and trying to walk
I wonder what she would be saying if she could talk
I'll know all about that when she reaches her two's

25

SUMMER STORM

Golf clubs are coming out of the garage or the basement. People are driving by waving and honking their horns, robins are gathering grass and sticks for their nests. Green leaves are popping out of, used to be, dead branches. The sky is blue with fluffy cumulous white clouds. A grey squirrel is chasing another squirrel up a tree and jumping over to other branches. You can hear the sounds of lawn mowers up and down the street. Children of every age are making the most of this sunny, warm day. You can smell the aroma from lilac bushes. The colors are breathtaking. White, purple or pink is what I can see from here. People stop to talk to their neighbors. Ball games are going on across the street. I hear of a ball game going on at the park. Families are enjoying being together to worship the Lord and then have a big barbecue together afterwards. Dandelions are trying to take over our lawn and other neighbors' yards. The sparrows are showing up in flocks as they fly down close to the birdfeeder to peck whatever is left behind from the other birds and the cats and squirrels.

I'm walking down the street with our granddaughters and we see a baby crying in the carriage. He is letting mom know he is awake and wants to eat or drink something now. Tantalizing smells of steaks, hamburgers and even hot dogs cooking on barbecues, make us hungry as we walk along.

People are washing their cars, to clean them up, after experiencing a rain storm yesterday. The girls and I are talking and walking faster as we are anxious to play in the sand at the beach. A few more blocks and they will be climbing on the jungle gym and swinging on the swings and possibly playing in the sand with me. We pass a couple pulling their son in a wagon. I think they have the same idea as we have. We can see the lake. It's just over there by the ice cream shop, as the girls lovingly refer to it. The girls are getting excited. We are going to have a great time in the hot sun. Other families will be there too making good use of a wonderful warm day.

The girls let out an energetic scream. We are here and it has been a long time coming. We haven't been together for months and they are really looking forward to spending some time with me, their Grandma.

I felt a rain drop on my arm. Oh no! This can't be happening.

All of a sudden the sun disappears and the sky gets dark and the clouds look angry. I look at the girls already nicely playing and inform them that we better get home and soon. With a little hesitation, they gather their things, including our picnic basket, and we strike out in the direction of home.

Things are suddenly changing for the worst. Mother's are calling their kids into their houses. People are running from the beach. We are included in that scene. It is several blocks and we have to make it home before the thunder and lightening takes over. Birds are gathering and heading for cover from the storm. The breeze is now a strong wind. We are running. I am ahead for now however the girls are fast catching up. I encourage them to keep coming we have to get home before there is a down pour. None of us are dressed for a storm. At least we have our jackets with us. That was a wise decision on Grandma's part. We are doing great. Obviously we are getting home a lot faster than when we were walking to the beach. The girls are getting tired, as a matter of fact so am I. We'll be home soon, I reassure them.

Trees are bending in the wind now. Debris is being blown around. Thank goodness we are almost home.

"There is the house girls! Can you see it, amongst all the beautiful green trees?

"Yes Grandma we can see it and we're sure happy your home is close."

We make it home, we are still puffing, from running, however we make it home and we are just wet, not soaked to the skin.

I am looking down at the girls as they hurry up to the bathroom to strip off their wet clothes. They are smiling. In fact they are laughing.

They holler down from the stairs to me, "that was fun Grandma that was really fun."

I turn to them and say," Yes girls that was fun. You know why it was fun for me?"

"Why?" They ask.

"It was fun for me because we are all home safe and sound, and that's what is very important to me."

We look out the window and to our amazement the wind is really strong now. There is nobody on the street. Everybody has run for cover. The rain is coming down in sheets and there is even some hail stones hitting the car. Branches lay broken and lying on the street. Some shingles are ripping off the house tops because of the strong cruel wind. The happy sounds of children at play are being replaced with sounds that are not so happy.

It started out being such a beautiful day and with everyone doing what they were enjoying. The day is quickly ending with the opposite reaction. The sky has turned grey and angry and is demanding people to stay in their houses or in a safe place, out of harms way.

"Great job girls! We left the beach when it was wise to and brought you home to your mom and dad safe and sound. Grandpa seems happy to see us too, although he doesn't say much, just smiles a lot."

26

TRUST IN HIM

"Honey would you get the phone please?"
"Why Barb? It will be for you anyway."
"No problem, Bill I'll get it."
It's Yvonne and her voice sounds different.
"Hi Mum, how are you doing to-day?"
"Great! What's up Yvonne? You sound sad."
"I'm concerned about your best friend .She's asking people on Face book to pray for her. She's having mixed emotions because her oldest son is striking off on his own for a job in Alberta. She's happy that he has made a decision to try something different."

She went on to say," Mum maybe you'd like to give Robin a call. I'm sure she'd appreciate your concern."

I assured Yvonne that I would definitely give her a call as soon as I tidied up the kitchen and finished the supper dishes.

The phone rings.
"Hi! Barb.
"Oh hi Robin I was just going to give you a call. How is Bradie doing? I was awoken quite a bit last night praying for a safe trip for him."
"That's kind of why I'm calling."
"Have you been crying? What's wrong?"
"I've been praying all day and most of the night myself. I'm trusting in Him to guide Bradie safely to the Camp.

Bradie phoned me from his cell."

He thinks he made a mistake he wants to turn around and come back home. He is very cross with me, he can't find the Camp and he wants to go to Red Deer and drop off whatever his cousin needs and then he will drive back home.

I told him "He needs to stay the course and follow through with what he had planned as other people are counting on him now. He is really angry. He is also so tired and full of questions of what he might expect when he gets to the Camp. Everything is so new and fresh. I feel sad that he is having such a rough time however I really have a peace about it. I'm sure he'll be just fine when he gets there and gets settled."

"That is a long way for a young man in his little black truck to drive all the way to the oil rigs in the camp in Alberta. What is that camp called anyway? I know I've never heard of it before. It's a good thing I'm not trying to find it."

"Where is he Robin? Is he safe and warm?"

"He is right now as we speak. He's been driving all day and night and he can't find the camp. He's in the bush now and can't see any sign of a Camp."

My heart sank. I was supposed to be the one to encourage her. My mind went reeling back to when Bradie was a little guy in my day-care and oh, what a sweetie. He was always quiet and had such a sweet disposition. He was quite timid and needed lots of love and encouragement. This was very easy for us to give him from our home.

I yanked my thoughts back to my talk with Robin.

My intention was to be strong for her however I could feel my heart throbbing.

Robin said, "Barb we have to trust God. He is the only One who can help him."

I reminded her that Bradie gave his life to Jesus when he was five-years-old. He was with me at the Terry Winter's gathering here in Killarney at the arena.

"I know he did Barb. I just hope he remembers that now

when he is so totally alone. He would realize he's really not alone at all."

Robin went on to say. "Barb I don't know what to do I feel so helpless. That's our son out in the middle of nowhere and when he phones for sympathy I just know that I have to tell him to move forward. Oh it's so hard being a Mom. You know Barb I have this beautiful peace in my heart so I'm certain I'm doing the right thing."

"That is absolutely so wonderful, I reassured her, God is bigger than any challenges or obstacles we will face."

I said a prayer over the entire family and she commented that she knew she did the right thing by phoning me.

"Has Bradie been in touch with his cousin? I'm sure he'd be able to help him find his way to the camp."

"He doesn't want to ask him how to get there. He wants to make it there on his own if he is going to get there."

More prayer needed. Let's pray for somebody to find him and lead him to the Camp. We did that over the phone.

"Just a minute Barb I think my husband's home. We'll talk about this and figure out where to go from here. I'll call you later."

I hung up the phone and with tears streaming down my cheeks I walked into the living-room to talk to my husband.

"What if that was one of our boys lost and alone in a bush in the pitch dark, with only trees around him? What if he runs out of gas in his truck? He's probably hungry. I know he's exhausted and cross with the world." He doesn't have a big amount of money."

"What should we do Bill? How can we help?"

"Do what you always do" trust in Him" like you do with every situation. Bill went on to say, he'll be fine you'll see."

I dried my eyes and proceeded to ask God for forgiveness.

Bill was right. That is what we must continue to do. God answers prayers. Amen and amen.

The phone was ringing. I picked it up and Robin was on

the other end.

"Hi Barb, this is Robin. I've got some good news. Bradie just phoned us. He found the Camp himself. He is having something to eat as we speak. He's in a nice cozy room with an inviting bed. He'll have a really good sleep and everything will look so much rosier when he wakes up for work in the morning."

"Thank-you Jesus for putting your "wall of protection" around Bradie and for bringing him safely to his destination." I whispered.

"Yes, replied Robin, thank-you Jesus for watching over our son."

"I'll let you go now Barb. We're all going to have a peaceful, beautiful sleep tonight. I know Bradie sure will and I am quite relieved myself.

27

CARMEN

The door opens. Eight year old Carmen is home from school. The children are happy to see her. She takes her coat off and quickly grabs her school bag.

She plunks down on the dark blue bean bag chair and makes herself real cozy as she shares. The children are excited and of course 3 year old Brooklyn wants to hold Carmen's new toys and things. I don't know what's being said however I can see the older ones are quite upset about the idea of Brooklyn touching Carmen's things. Brooklyn starts to cry.

Carmen reaches over and puts Brooklyn on her knee as she talks softly to her. It looks like she's got another surprise to show the kids. Brooklyn has now stopped crying as she touches Carmen's face.

"I like your shirt she tells Carmen. I like how it's blue and green and all mixed up" says Brooklyn.

"Yes, that's called a tie dyed shirt, replies a soft spoken Carmen.

"Your pants are black and soft, they are so cozy," says her new found friend.

"Oh look! she hollers to the rest of the kids, "Carmen has blue and green striped soft socks, her socks look like the same colors as her shirt."

3 year old, Brooklyn turns upside down on the bean bag

A Book of LOVE

chair so she can put her face on Carmen's soft socks.

The children all laugh.

Carmen shows the children something she made at home.

"Do you want me to show you guys how I made this?"

"Oh yes!" was the resounding reply.

Carmen proceeded to talk to them.

"First you need a pipe cleaner. Now, see these beads they are called Mickey Mouse beads."

She went on explaining. "Decide now what you are going to make and then cut off the length you need. Now you must bend the pipe cleaner at the bottom so the beads will not fall off. As you can see these are red and white beads and I'm going to make a candy cane for my Christmas tree at home.

The children were excited watching her make something. She carefully threaded the pretty beads on the pipe cleaner.

She had lots of help, naturally, from the excited children circling around her.

The kids took turns handing her the beautiful, red and white, tiny beads.

The beads gathered, on the candy cane while the wide eyed youngsters kept looking at me in disbelief. She twisted the top and showed them the finished candy cane.

She thanked the children for helping and ran and put it in her special bag to take home to display on the Christmas tree at home.

28

BILL'S STORY

I was born in my grandfather's house in s'gravendel Holland on Feb 1st 1945 to Arie and Elizabeth Van Der Stel My family was living under German occupation at the time. I have two younger siblings. Cobi was born Dec 3rd 1946 and my brother Henry was born Sept 23rd 1948.

My mom was very sick when Henry was born. The doctor was upstairs with my Mom and it seemed like everybody else could see her but they wouldn't let me. This made me feel very left out and I was scared that something really bad was going to happen to her.

My dad worked at a flax processing company. They made linen out of the flax sheaves. The paper was also used in Bibles. Flax paper was slow to burn so it made good cigarette paper.

Some of the fun times I remember were my mom and dad taking us for rides on their bikes to visit people. My dad would take Henry and me and my mom would take our sister Cobi. A favorite ride was eighteen kilometers away and that was to my Grandma's. When I turned eight I pedaled my own bike to their house and back that distance.

Another fun time I remember was when we rode to the ocean. A big white sandy beach was exciting for us to play on plus there were rides such as a roller coaster and bumping cars to go on. I wanted to ride them myself however mom wouldn't let me she figured her six year old boy was too young to do that by himself.

Although mom did the disciplining in our home, she also taught me how to tie my shoes and make certain knots in ropes and neat things like that. Mom did all the baking as she didn't want me to get burned on the wood stove she was using. We used to burn peat moss instead of coal.

Mom would get us all dressed up for Church on Sunday and we all went together. Mom used to sing in the choir and my dad played the trumpet in the fireman's band.

My mom made all our clothes as well as knit all our socks, sweaters scarves and mitts.

Our meals consisted mainly of beans and potatoes. In the summer time we added a few more vegetables to our meals.

I remember mom making a lunch for me. She would put it in a cloth bag and I would go with my neighbor, a friend of Mom's and Dad's. We would go out to the farms and load up the big truck with vegetables and then come in and deliver them to the people in the City.

Much to my mother's surprise I recall when I was two years old. I was riding on the front of my dad's bike and a young woman whizzed by us screaming as she was in a wagon with a runaway team of horses. Somebody finally caught up with her and rescued her. It left quite an impression on me as I was so young at the time.

My grandfather (my mother's step-dad) kept racing pigeons. He separated them and only kept the best, which meant he destroyed the others. My grandfather on my Dad's side raised rabbits and chickens for food. Most people could not afford meat.

In our area of town there were big trucks loaded with sugar beets and when they would take the corner too fast sugar beets would be strewn out on the street. I would collect them and bring them over to my grandfather's place and he would give me a quarter for them.

A Book of LOVE

When I was five I had a scooter. For hours I rode it up and down the street.

One day I ran out of the house and right onto the street and a motor cycle was driving by and it hit me. The driver of the bike felt awful and helped me gather myself up. I took off running in the house and up the stairs into my bed. Of course mom went up after me and noticed blood running out of my ear. She took me to the doctor's house as there were no hospitals.

Every morning early the milk man would come to the houses. One day I got up early, nobody in our family was out of bed yet. I decided to go for a ride with the milkman without telling anybody. This turned out to be not the best decision as mom couldn't find me and was quite upset when she did and of course relieved that I was safe.

A tiny truck with three wheels, one on the front and two on the back, and a roof over the top of the truck, used to pedal fresh fish. The big flat fish my parents used to buy was my favorite and they used to make delicious fries to go with it.

Another thing I remember was an organ grinder going down the street. This was a big thing on four wheels with a guy turning the wheel with a big handle on the side to play music to entertain the people living along the street.

The Queen's birthday was a big celebration in our home town. They would play on the bandstand in the middle of the creek in the evening. Alongside the creek were banks that were grass and fence posts with paper lanterns on the posts. These were orange since that was the Queen's colors in the house of orange. The kids used to walk around carrying paper lanterns with a candle on the end of a stick. In the daytime they had an exciting soccer game for all to enjoy. My dad used to play the trumpet at this celebration.

I started school in Holland. Grades 1 and 2 two people sat in one desk as the desks were very wide. The books were kept under the desk. The books we had in Grade 1 were very colorful with bright pictures. The story was about a cat named "Tom." The school was along the creek with a very small yard for playing outside. This yard was all cobblestones.

There was no space for a garden at our home so my dad rented a plot, outside of town to plant one. When I was supposed to be helping him I was eating someone else's strawberries from another garden plot. When it was time to go home my dad would ride his bike holding on with one hand so he could carry a gunny sack of potatoes on his back. I rode on the back of his bike.

Sunday afternoon as a family we would go down to the river and have a big picnic. There were aunts and uncles and my cousin. My dad and uncles would try to teach my mom and my aunts how to swim. They would tie a rope around their waist and then they would hold the rope ready to pull them out if they ran into trouble. While this was going on me and my cousin would be catching frogs and throwing them at my mom and my aunts and listen to them scream.

On February 1st, 1953 there was a terrible storm on the north sea. The wind was so strong it made the wall paper inside our house flap. The dikes broke and the water came in the houses. My dad carried my mother, who was terrified of the water and us kids to the neighbors as their house was higher so we'd be out of danger. Dad waded through ice-cold water in order to do this. We went upstairs. This was my birthday so my mom and my aunts made me a birthday cake on a kerosene stove. The wood stove in the kitchen was under water. Our house had water up to the ceiling.

In a couple of days we were evacuated. We climbed out of a window in the porch onto a plank and we had to walk from the roof to the dike. The American army from Germany came to Holland to help out with their amphibious vehicles to help with the evacuation and the stranded people. We were evacuated to Rotterdam and we were billeted with a couple in an apartment building. They had two girls around my age. They had the luxury of running water a shower and an inside toilet. This was a nice change for us. I can remember the lunches and the drinks were also a lot better than we had back home.

They fixed the dikes then they pumped the water out with humongous pumps. My dad went back to look for bodies and help with the clean-up. Fifty-two people died from that flood in our hometown. The dad's were pulling up their own dead children.

The first day back home my mom made supper on the wood stove that was now out on the side walk. I sat on a wooden chair and fell as the chair was rotten from the water.

We lost everything we had so the Dutch Government paid our way to Canada. We could have gone to Australia, South Africa or the United States but my dad chose Canada because the Canadian army played a significant role in liberating Holland from the German's in the Second World War.

We received all kinds of medical tests after meeting with the Canadian Officials.

Before we left on the ship we went around and visited all our relatives to say good-bye. I was eight- years-old so to me this was a big adventure and I couldn't understand why everybody was crying.

When the big day came they had all of our belongings in a big crate and we left on a bus to the port with some of our relatives.

I can remember being on the ship and waving down at our relatives as they were waving up to us. This was not a fancy ship. My dad was in a dorm with a bunk bed with me and my brother and my mother was in another dorm with my sister Cobi.

The first night I was sea sick. The constant motion made me nauseated. The next day we went for meals and we had to take a life boat drill. We learned how to put on a life jacket and we had to know which boat we had to go to incase there was some disaster.

We ate in the big dining hall three times a day and I can still remember we could drink as much milk as we wanted and we had ice-cream for desert. There was a movie theatre in the ship where they showed cartoons for the kids. This ship was called SSWaterman. One day I was aware of something big in the water. It could have been a whale or a dolphin or something like that.

On July 30th, 1953 seven days after we left we landed in Halifax on Pier 21 which is now a famous museum. People travel from all over the world to see it. We had to go through customs and deal with the immigration again. Now we are in Canada.

We got on the train and it took us 5 days to get to Winnipeg. There were so many train stops on the way. The soot from the steam engine made my mom very upset as she couldn't keep us clean and that was very important to her.

When we arrived in Winnipeg a Dutch farmer met us and took us to the place where we were supposed to live. He told us it was a nice house. When we got there it turned out to be a square one-room shack which had a big hole in the center of the floor where the Natives had their fire and along one wall were rabbit cages.

We went back to Winnipeg and stayed at the Immigration Hall, beside the railway station. We were there for two or three days. We kids played on the Emperos of Dufferin which was an old steam locomotive in front of the railway station.

My dad was supposed to get a job in Choiceland, Sk. When we arrived there was no house for us so we stayed in an empty granary that night. It was August so it wasn't that cold and we all managed to get through it. Our next stop was Silver Park, Sk. There we had a shack like a chicken house. The whole family slept in one bed. We were there for four months so we had to go to school.

My dad got a job in Melfort, SK. Working for a dairy farmer. This house had 2 bedrooms and a big living room and kitchen combined. I remember at threshing time I got to ride a big work horse to take him to the creek to give him a drink. The school I attended in Melfort was just across the street from our home.

In August 1955 we moved to Saskatoon where we lived on a feed lot south of Saskatoon where my dad worked. We walked a mile and a half to Thorton School.

In 1959 I started high school at Sask Tech Collegiate.

My dad ended up in the hospital with a back injury in 1962 and a guy that was his room-mate suggested I should join the air Force. I got my citizenship papers before this. I joined the Air Force reserve in June 1962. The summer of 62 I went to Trenton, Ontario with the Air Force. In the summer of 63 I was training rookies in shops in the Air force.

In the spring of 63 I met Miss Barbara Allen. She was going with my friend Keith who I met in the reserve as he joined up the same time I did. Barbara was working at the Telephone office in Saskatoon. She later joined up as a clerk typist so the three of us were together a lot of the time. We even went on a trip together later to BC. We had a great time and I ended up driving the car most of the time.

In the fall of 1963 we moved to 803 Wilson Crescent, which was where Keith and his family lived. I finished high school in 1964 and went to work at Western Automotive Rebuilders, rebuilding engines.

In 1965 I worked in a welding shop. I was machining and welding farm equipment and doing repair work Barb married Keith in 66 and had a little boy Kevin. It broke my heart as I was in love with her too. I told my mother if I couldn't marry Barb I wouldn't marry anybody. Barb's Mum passed away on Sept.9th 1969. She was devastated. I was definitely in the party crowd or even when there wasn't a crowd. Timothy was born on Jan.27th 1970 and I looked after

Kevin while she was in the hospital. In June 1970 Barb left Keith and went to the farm. The divorce went through.

Fast forward my life I married Barbara in Dec 19th, 1970 I was very happy, and my life changed forever. I adopted her two boys Kevin and Timothy and now we are a family with lots of responsibilities. I loved the boys and Barb very much. With all the challenges Barb went through in her past life, she ended up in severe depression which I helped her get through. In 1972 Barb and I had a precious little baby girl Larissa, who was born without a right hand. We all loved her so very much. We now had a girl in our family, a whole new ballgame. She became very independent very fast.

I got a job in Lanigan, Sask.working in a Potash mine. Barb was very sick and needed help with her appointments and the kids as she couldn't do it herself. In a few years later we moved back to the home base. We were expecting again which we were excited about. We were secretly hoping for another baby girl, a best-friend for Larissa. On Jan 19th, 1976 we had our baby girl Yvonne. This was double excitement as she was born on my mom's birthday.

Moving right along I was offered a position of managing a Co-op Implements store in Killarney, MB. I left the family at home and went and checked it out. On Dec 1979 we moved to Killarney. This was very hard on Barb and the kids as all that was familiar to them we left in Saskatchewan. Friends, relatives, school and school friends were all left behind.

My responsibility rested on building up this store so family life got left out. Their mother was there though for them every step of the way.

This position was rough going and in three years I quit. I've been working at the Royal Canadian Legion. First I worked for the Legion and now for the past 30 years I've managed it. In the same period I was in the Fire Dept for 10 years and was in the ambulance for 5 years. I quit both when I turned 50.

A Book of LOVE

In 2002 my dad passed away the same day our first granddaughter Lindsay was born. I gave my life to the Lord in 2002 and was baptized in the Killarney Lake on the 1st of Sept that same year.

I've been very busy: Things need fixing. The rooms in our house needed renovating. Meetings to go to and sports on T.V. Time spent surfing on the computer, work at the Legion, looking after the yard, planting the garden and all the outside work for every season, being married and having 4 children and lots of grand-children and on and on it goes. The last project we did was renovated the music room into an inviting room for Barb to do her writing course, which is her latest project. She really likes it. She has her own writing desk and chair and has room for all her books and binders and Bibles and the computer is there for us to share. All the things are handy.

I haven't taken much time in my life to relax and have fun. That time will come soon I hope. Barb keeps reminding me, how important it is to have fun, while we're young at heart. As a matter of fact we have been invited on a cruise with Kevin and Anita and the girls in August. Barb and her sisters are planning a trip in August.

It is 2012. Kevin and Anita are married and have Lindsay and Ashley. Larissa and Christopher are married and have two girls Caitlyn, and Juliana, which are a real blessing. Yvonne and Glenn are married with two girls Tia and Danica, beautiful smart girls and now Timothy and Sherri are married and they brought us two teen-agers and several foster kids which are beautiful and special. Right now in their family they have Gregory Kara and Leila, Hasen, Corina and just lately Eva. They will probably be loving and caring for a lot more as the time goes by. Their heart goes out to hurting kids. We have many grand children which we love and possibly there will be more in the future. Barb and I have been married a short 41 years and still going strong. Barb loves children. She has been running a day-care in our home for going on 22 years. We've had our ups and downs however we have the Lord we can count on and we do give our cares to Him. We are deeply loved, truly blessed and highly favored. Thank- you Jesus

29

A VISUAL MIRACLE

In March the 12th of 1996 I gave my life to the Lord and on the 29th of July 1996, I got baptized in the Killarney Lake in Killarney. There were signs up all over the Park warning us not to go in the water. Brent Denham, who baptized me, went in with me in the water and the water separated. We were free to get baptized in the clean water. We were out on the grass for a few minutes and then the rain poured down on us and everybody that was watching. At the time though when I was receiving my baptism it was a gorgeous day and what an emotional time that was for me.

I was tired and not feeling like going anywhere, when my son phoned me from Brandon, Mb.

"Hi Mum."

"Hello, I replied," What's up with you phoning me this time of night?"

"Mum, I was asked to go to this healing service at Calvary temple. I've been going this past week. It is really amazing what I have seen with my own eyes."

"Tell me about it." I said.

"Mum could you come in tomorrow night at 7:00 p.m. and I'll meet you there. "I just want you to see it for yourself."

I didn't really want to go however I hadn't been feeling good for quite awhile and I figured what harm would it do. It would make Timothy happy. Timothy was feeling a little overwhelmed.

I went and met our son at the Church on Friday evening to watch people receiving healing for all kinds of ailments.

Being a brand new Christian, who had been hungrily reading the Bible, I was very excited about watching these miracles take place. It said in the Bible that Jesus travelled and healed all that were sick or afflicted I was watching the Word of the Lord working in this place and my son, Timothy, and I were truly amazed.

During the part of the evening the Pastor was telling us about a healing he himself had received. He said he was working under his car. He had the car jacked up, the jack slipped and the car came down on him and crushed his glasses and tore up his face quite a bit. He rolled out from under the car and began to believe Jesus for his healing. He told us that he experienced a miracle. Not only was his head and face healed but he prayed for his eye sight.

He said, "He couldn't afford to buy new glasses." His eye sight was restored and he never had to buy any more glasses.

"Faith comes by hearing and hearing by the word of GOD" I was so new at being a Christian I had child-like faith and I thought God is no respecter of persons. I read what He'll do for one He'll do for all. It also says God is the same yesterday, today and forever. I prayed when I got home. I asked the Lord to heal my eyes. It seemed like my glasses were coming apart or out of shape or one of my kids had stepped on them and broken them. I simply with child-like faith believed God would heal my eyes as he did that mans' I just heard about at Church.

After that short prayer, I began to feel Him working on my eyes. My eyes were opening up and it felt like little fingers were on my eyes. I knew my prayer was answered. I was going to the Church in Killarney the following day and while I was walking something nudged me that I should go back and put on my glasses. I stopped and said out loud.

"NO, I am not!" Faith without doubting! I heard that Pastor speak in his sermon. You must not doubt once God has healed you. I kept walking towards the Church and once again the enemy was trying to make me go back and get my glasses. I stopped and said once again out loud.

"I am not going back, Jesus has healed my eyes and it is finished"

I got to the Church and excitedly went in and went to some other believers whom I felt close to and shared my miracle with them. We rejoiced together. It is 2012 and I have never worn a pair of glasses since that spring day in March. Praise the Lord. God is good all the time.

30

RESCUED BY ANGELS

"Timothy what are you doing phoning me, I thought you were on holidays with your friend, Mark?"

"I just wanted to hear your voice Mum."

"What is that supposed to mean son?"

"Actually I want to hear everybody I loves' voice," said a different sounding Timothy.

I said, "Why in the world are you talking like this you are scaring me?"

"It's O.K. now Mum I'm safe."

Here is Timothy's true story.

It was 11:00 in the morning on a Friday and my holidays were slipping by fast so I left my friend sleeping. My dog, Rocky, and I went for a walk. Then I got the bright idea we should go canoeing. My plan was to stay in the shallow end as I'd never done this before and I didn't even know how to swim very well. I was having a quiet time enjoying being in the outdoors and the sunshine and with my dog Rocky, when a "mad boater" starts aiming his motor boat directly at my canoe. This guy was drunk so I decided to move my canoe "just a wee bit" deeper so that I would be able to avoid him.

Before I knew it the combination of my intentional paddling and the waves from his boat brought me out to the area where there was no shelter from the wind. I was instantly swept out towards the middle of Lake Winnipeg. I tried to head back to shore but it was not happening.

The more I tried, the farther I would go the wrong way. A storm was brewing and there was a real possibility that if I did not get out of there lightening would hit me. I tried everything. I prayed, I yelled, I screamed out to Jesus. I was so scared and I went through every emotion that you can go through. I started trying to deal with the fact that I would die out there and that I better make sure I was ready. I tried to figure out how painful it would be to swallow that much water. I even thought of just giving up.

I then got a burst of motivation and decided I would jump into the water and drag the canoe. This did not work. The more I swam, the more hopeless the situation seemed.

"Timothy, this sounds like a nightmare, who helped you?"

"Just listen Mum, I'll tell you"

Once again, terror set in and I tried to figure out how in the world I was supposed to keep my head when death seemed so imminent.

The next thing I remember was a boat pulling up beside me and a very concerned group of fishermen dragging me and my dog, over the edge of their boat and out of the water. They explained that it would be far too dangerous to try to rescue the sinking canoe and that we would have to go back for it when the weather permitted, if it was still there. Then they covered me in blankets and shared with me how they came to find me. They explained that they were the only boat on the lake and that they themselves were going home for the day because the lake had become too rough and dangerous to justify staying out there. Some special person on the boat insisted they go over and check out where I was. Thank God for him.

The next day I picked up the canoe from the coastguard's

headquarters. They told me they found the canoe three miles out from shore and that I was lucky to be alive. I got the names and addresses of the fishermen, who had saved me, but when I attempted to find them to say thank-you, they were no-where to be found.

What an awesome feeling to know that God cares so intimately about us that He would send angels to rescue us in our time of need. GOD DID NOT FORGET ABOUT ME!!!!!! What a Great God!!

"Timothy that was amazing. Thank-you Jesus for putting angels around our son"

My husband Bill and I live in Killarney, MB in a 117 year- old 2 storey cozy stone house on a double lot with big old oak trees lilac bushes and other trees around our yard with a small space for a garden. We have lived here since 1979. Our children were brought up here. Yvonne, our youngest daughter, was 3 years-old when we moved to Killarney. The kids went to school and made friends and we had a good time watching them grow and play and learn. As every parent feels, they grow up way too fast and then they are gone and you hope you've taught them the important things in life so they can carry on with their own. I worked outside of our home when they were little however I always made time to listen to them and encourage them the best I could. When the kids graduated and moved away, I filled our home with day-care kids.

This is 2012 and our home is still ringing with laughter and happy noises from the kids here in the day-care. The babies and all the other children are dearly loved and cared for. The children are taught to love and respect me and I love and care for and respect each of them. We have a great time sharing and learning from each other, especially when the children get a little bigger like 1year –old to 5 years-old. When they start school, I don't see them as much however they come after school for a snack and play until their parents come for them.

Bill and I and Laddie, my 9 year -old little shitsui dog, are very happy here in this wonderful little town of Killarney. We attend New Life Assembly Church and have a real support group here. Our 4 children and their spouses and their families all live in Winnipeg. MB. We try to get together as often as possible as nobody could love them more than we do and they know it.

I took a risk and sent away for a writing course, 2 years ago, which I worked at for 2 years letting the Lord lead me as I never had any idea how I was going to accomplish this. I was already busy with the full time day-care and everyday life here at home. What other big plans He has for me, I'm not sure. I do know however it will be good.

I can do all things through Christ who strengthens me. Phil 4:13.

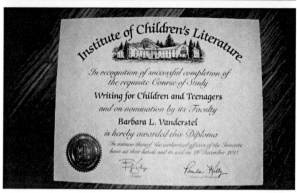

CPSIA information can be obtained at www.ICGtesting.com
Printed in the USA
BVOW021219030412

286746BV00001B/6/P